MW00604383

COMPLETE KICKING

THE ULTIMATE GUIDE TO KICKS FOR MARTIAL ARTS
SELF-DEFENSE & COMBAT SPORTS

OTHER TITLES BY THE AUTHOR

BOOKS
Power Breathing
Vital Point Strikes
Ultimate Flexibility
Ultimate Fitness Through Martial Arts
Combat Strategy
The Art of Harmony
Teaching Martial Arts: The Way of The Master
Martial Arts Instructor's Desk Reference
1,001 Ways To Motivate Yourself & Others
Martial Arts After 40
Complete Taekwondo Poomsae
Taekwondo Kyorugi: Olympic Style Sparring
Muye Dobo Tongji: The Comprehensive Illustrated Manual of Martial Arts of Ancient Korea
Taekwondo Taegeuk Poomsae
Taekwondo Self-defense
Taekwondo Step Sparring

COMPLETE KICKING

THE ULTIMATE GUIDE TO KICKS FOR MARTIAL ARTS
SELF-DEFENSE & COMBAT SPORTS

SANG H. KIM, PH.D.

 Turtle Press   Washington DC

COMPLETE KICKING

A Turtle Press Book / 2009

Copyright © 2009 Sang H. Kim. All Rights Reserved.

Printed in the United States of America. No part of this book may be reproduced without written permission except in the case of brief quotations embodied in articles or reviews.

For information, address Turtle Press, 500 N. Washington St #1545, Rockville MD 20849
www.TurtlePress.com

Photographer: Marc Regis, Cynthia A. Kim
Photo models: Sang H. Kim, Kyu-hyung Lee, Carlos Sanchez, Marco Corea

ISBN 9781934903131
LCCN 2009012831
Printed in the United States of America

Warning-Disclaimer

This book is designed to provide information on specific skills used in martial arts and fitness training. It is not the purpose of this book to reprint all the information that is otherwise available to the author, publisher, printer or distributors, but instead to complement, amplify and supplement other texts. You are urged to read all available material, learn as much as you wish about the subjects covered in this book and tailor the information to your individual needs. Anyone practicing the skills presented in this book should be physically capable to do so and have the permission of a licensed physician before participating in this activity or any physical activity.

Every effort has been made to make this book as complete and accurate as possible. However, there may be mistakes, both typographical and in content. Therefore, this text should be used only as a general guide and not the ultimate source of information on the subjects presented here in this book on any skill or subject. The purpose of this book is to provide information and entertain. The author, publisher, printer and distributors shall neither have liability nor responsibility to any person or entity with respect to loss or damages caused, or alleged to have been caused, directly or indirectly, by the information contained in this book.

Library of Congress Cataloguing in Publication Data
Kim, Sang H.
Complete kicking : the ultimate guide to kicks for martial arts self-defense & combat sports / by Sang H. Kim.
    p. cm.
ISBN 978-1-934903-13-1
1. Martial arts--Training. 2. Self-defense--Training. I. Title.
GV1101.K52 2009
796.8--dc22
                        2009012831

CONTENTS

INTRODUCTION

KEY POINT

Kicking is for every fighter. It's powerful, fast, and deadly. Regardless of martial art style, the fundamentals are much the same: kick fast, kick hard, kick precisely. To meet these goals, you need to train your body, strengthen your muscles, and condition your mind.

You'll be surprised to find initially how natural kicking is, just like walking and running. However, to excel at kicking, you have to go beyond what is natural. You must learn to control your body at all times in order to acquire precision, speed and power. Then your body will become a deadly weapon for self-protection and an invincible tool for sport competition.

After you perfect the basic skills, you are only a few steps away from mastering challenging advanced kicks. As you progress and learn increasingly difficult kicks, you will find that practicing kicking enhances your mental clarity and concentration, as well as your physical fitness.

Left: Sang H. Kim, performing twist kick, Kukkiwon, Seoul, Korea

PREPARATION

If you're reading this book, you obviously have a serious interest in improving your kicking skills. You might already be a martial arts student or you might be thinking of taking up a martial art. Either way, here are some key things to know before you get started:

FIND A PLACE

Kicking can be practiced almost anywhere that has a flat surface clear of obstacles. You can practice on your own, but if you are novice, professional instruction at a martial art school or program is recommended. To choose a class, visit the school(s) you are interested in and see for yourself: Is the instructor professional and knowledgeable? Do you feel like learning from him or her? Do the students have the right attitude? Check out the condition of the facility - is it clean and safe? Ask students what they like and don't like about the class. Once you're settled, either in a class or at home, develop a regular training schedule to achieve your goals.

PROPER OUTFIT

Kicking requires free range of movement, so your training outfit should be loose fitting, especially in the hips and knees. Loose fitting shorts (1), sweat pants or a martial art uniform are safe, comfortable options.

EQUIPMENT

In the beginning stage of learning a kick, you may need something to assist with your balance and posture, such as a stretching bar, chair, or even a wall (2). Once you've mastered the basic method of kicking, you'll use a target to improve your precision. Commonly used targets are a speed-bag hung from the ceiling, a free standing reflex bag, a double end ball or a hand target (3) held by a partner. For power and speed practice, you'll use a heavy bag (4).

SAFETY

Before practicing a new kick, learn the movement and visualize it. Know your physical limits and build from where you are. Gradually increase the height, speed, power and complexity of your movements. It is also very important to warm up for 10 to 15 minutes prior to practice and to cool down for about 5 minutes afterward to prevent injuries.

A FIRST LESSON

FIGHTING STANCE

Your stance is the position of your feet and hands. To make a basic fighting stance:

1. Place your feet about shoulder width apart with your weak side foot in front and your strong side foot in the rear. (If you're right handed, your right foot is your strong side.) For power, widen your stance. For speed and mobility, narrow your stance.

Foot position determines your kicking capacity and controls your center.

2. Turn your front foot inward 15° to 30° and turn your rear foot outward 60° to 90°. Keep your weight slightly more on the balls of your feet.

3. Bend your knees slightly.

4. Keep your torso upright and angled away from your opponent to protect your vital targets. Tuck your chin down slightly toward your chest and look at the target.

5. Bend your elbows and bring your hands in front of your chest to protect your torso and face.

6. Relax your shoulders and move rhythmically.

BALANCE

Your knee and head positions are critical for maintaining your balance. Keep your head level and look at the target. Keep your knees slightly flexed to lower your center of gravity. When you kick, your standing knee should remain slightly flexed to maintain your balance in motion.

CONTROL

Kicking requires you to have two contradictory attributes: control and freedom of movement. You need to control your body to execute a kick precisely. However, constant controlling, and the consciousness of it, makes your body stiff. Through practice, you will develop "muscle memory" so that eventually your body will perform the kick without conscious thought. Muscle memory allows you to focus on suppleness without controlling the "moving parts" of each kick.

PRACTICE

Don't be afraid to experiment with changes that might improve your performance. Vary your practice routine so it is mentally and physically engaging, not routine or boring. When you become good at in-place kicking, add footwork and drills or vary the speed, power and height.

FEEDBACK

When you run into trouble with a kick, listen to your body and go back to basics. Everyone's body is shaped and functions differently, so you might need to adapt the instructions in this book to fit your own body type. Problems are often the foundation for enhanced performance, so don't get discouraged. Stay positive and experiment.

REVISION

There are many levels of mastery and your perception of perfection fluctuates because your kicking changes according to your condition, opponent, and circumstances. In training, you'll find that you have to constantly revisit a time when a kick felt right for you and try to recapture that feeling and build on it.

DEVELOPING FORM

Form is the relationship of the key parts of the body illustrated at right. No matter how you alter your stance, the relationship of the four circled areas should remain constant. If you turn your hips 45°, then your chest and knees should move accordingly.

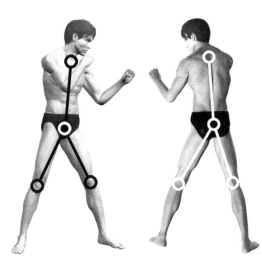

From the basic fighting stance, for example, your stance for each kick will be slightly different. Front kick begins from a conventional stance, but for side kick, your stance should be turned more to side to create a coiling force. As you bring your hip forward and knee up (photo 1), the body pivots (photo 2) and shoots the rear foot toward the target (photo 3). When you establish the correct form for your kick, your leg should naturally shoot along the most efficient path to the target.

3 STAGES OF FRONT KICK

1. READY	Position your feet shoulder width apart. Raise your hands in front of your torso. Relax your shoulders. Look forward. (1)
2. KICK	Bring your knee up (2a) and snap your foot forward toward the target (2b).
3. REPOSE	Retract your foot swiftly and prepare for your next action. (3)

1   2a   2b   3

ARM POSITION

To find the most natural position of your arms and hands, raise your arms higher than your usual fighting stance (left photo 1) and slowly lower them until you find the right height (photo 2). Keep your elbows bent and swing your arms around your torso a few times, then stop where you feel most comfortable. Make they cover the vital targets of the torso.

KNEE CONTROL

The knee travels straight forward in front kick, in a circular motion in roundhouse kick, backward in back kick. How you manipulate your knee determines the angle of the kick. You can practice knee control in most of the twelve directions of the clock.

3 KICKING ESSENTIALS

BASE

Your two feet form the base for your actions. The ideal base is about shoulder width or a bit wider. Positioning your feet too far apart or too close together creates an unstable base. Next, align your feet according to what type of kick you are planning to perform. For front kick, for instance, turn your feet forward. For side kick, align your feet sideways and parallel to each other. For roundhouse kick, turn your feet about 45°, between the positions of front kick and side kick.

PIVOT POINT

Your standing leg becomes a pivot point when you kick. If you do a roundhouse kick with your rear leg, your front leg is the pivot point. If you throw a front leg roundhouse kick, your rear leg is the pivot point. The pivot point plays an important role in kicking. The smoother you pivot, the better. The quicker you pivot, the more powerful your kick will be. The more stable your pivot is, the more precise your kick will be.

IMPACT

Impact results from a high velocity strike, or a low velocity strike with sufficient weight behind it. You can strike a target with your foot, knee, or shin. For effectiveness, your strike should be precise, fast, and penetrating. To further enhance the impact, strive for maximum range of motion of your kicks through stretching and greater focus of your physical and mental energy through proper breathing and yelling (kihap, kiai). Impact is the ultimate goal of kicking.

pivot point

Impact

base

3 ESSENTIAL ELEMENTS OF KICKING

With two feet on the ground, your base is strong. Shifting your weight forward and pivoting on the front foot results in a powerful impact.

HIGH IMPACT KICK
Improve your impact power through heavy bag training.

5 KICKING STAGES

READY

Before kicking, confirm that you have a strong base and align your feet according to what type of kick you are planning to use. Keep your arms close to your body in a guarding position and look at your target. Stay light on your feet and ready to move.

SHIFT

Before turning your body, shift your weight to your front leg for a rear leg kick or to your rear leg for a front leg kick. Do not change the height of your head or your facial expression when you shift your weight, because this will reveal your intentions to your opponent. Be calm and move subtly as you initiate your kick.

PIVOT

Your standing leg becomes a pivot point when you kick. Always pivot on the ball of your foot, raising your heel slightly to facilitate the pivot. As you pivot, chamber your kick by raising your knee into the appropriate position.

KICK

Impact results from a high velocity strike, so kick as quickly as you can while maintaining accuracy. Penetrate two to six inches into the target.

REPOSE

Retract your foot and leg swiftly and prepare for the next action, which might be another kick as part of a combination or a defensive reaction to your opponent's counterattack.

5 STAGES OF KICKING

amount of force used

repose   kick   pivot   shift   ready

REAR LEG KICK

Pivot 180°   Shift weight forward

FRONT LEG KICK

Pivot 90°   Shift weight backward

3 POWER GENERATORS

KNEE

Bending your knee prior to kicking is called chambering. The way you chamber your knee will determine the direction, range of motion and power of your kick. In general, where you point your knee is the direction of the force of your kick. The sharper you bend your knee, the more power you can generate due to a larger range of motion. If your chamber is lazy, your kick will lack power.

HIP

The hip is the primary mover of the body and it functions as a central powerhouse for kicking and punching. The muscles and bones of the hip are large and powerful and are the site of your center of gravity. By rotating your hip quickly and powerfully, you propel knee and foot into the target with maximum power. For many kicks, "snapping" your hip also adds to the impact power of your kick.

HEAD

The head is a stabilizer. By keeping your head upright, you anchor the alignment of your spine and maintain the pivoting power of the lower body around the central axis of the spine. If you drop your head while kicking, the force of your kick is dispersed, much like an uncoiled spring.

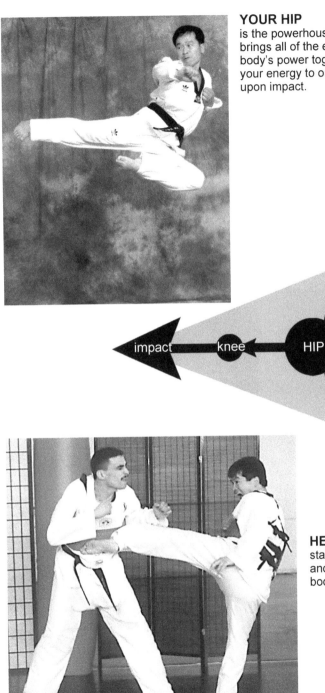

YOUR HIP

is the powerhouse for kicking. It brings all of the elements of your body's power together and directs your energy to one single point upon impact.

HEAD-UP

stabilizes your posture and integrates the body's force.

KICKING PHYSICS

In the science of kicking, there are three axes of the body: torso, thigh, and shin. Each transmits force and the further a point is from the origin of the force the more potential force it carries.

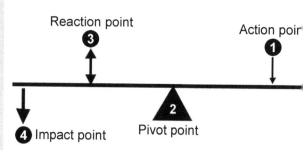

Reaction point

③

Action point

①

④ Impact point

② Pivot point

The initial point of action is called the **Action Point**.

The multiplying point of force is called the **Pivot Point,** where mechanical force is magnified.

The effect of applying the action point is called the **Reaction Point**.

The striking spot is called the **Impact Point**.

The primary pivot point in the body is the lower abdomen which facilitates force magnification between the action point and reaction point.

* The best exercise for strengthening the pivot point (abdomen) is sit-ups.

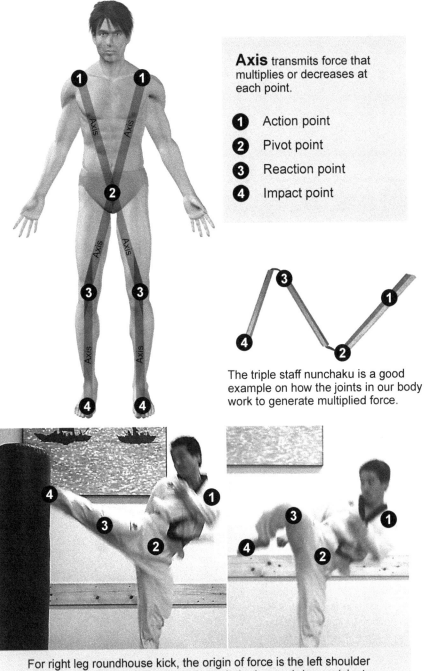

Axis transmits force that multiplies or decreases at each point.

1 Action point
2 Pivot point
3 Reaction point
4 Impact point

The triple staff nunchaku is a good example on how the joints in our body work to generate multiplied force.

For right leg roundhouse kick, the origin of force is the left shoulder (action point). The force passes through the lower abdomen (pivot point) and is magnified at the knee (reaction point) which propels the foot toward the target (impact point).

Sang H. Kim, demonstrating a full split, Glasgow, Scotland

UNDERSTANDING
THE BODY

To advance in kicking practice, it is important to have some basic knowledge of how the body works, particularly the bones, joints and muscles. They are the three primary mechanical devices that maximize the impact of your kicks. When you understand how they work, you can fully take advantage of what you have available. Not only will your training be more effective, but you'll be less susceptible to injury. If you don't understand how your body works, you might work hard but risk poor results and even injury. So take a few moments and review this chapter before you get started.

THE BODY STRUCTURE

THE TORSO

When your kicking form is correct, your torso stabilizes your body. If your form is incorrect, your torso can unbalance your body and reduce the power, height and speed of your kick. Because your torso is the heaviest and most cumbersome part of your body, it is important to keep it at the center of your movement and allow your arms and legs to rotate around the torso. Imagine that your torso is the eye of the hurricane of your movements.

THE SPINE

The spine is a complex network of muscles, ligaments, bones, joints, cartilage and nerves that work together to support and mobilize the body: support to stand, walk and lift; mobility for movements such as turning, twisting, bending, jumping and kicking. Because the spine is the primary support and movement structure of the torso, it is very important to stretch the back properly before and after kicking for optimal flexibility.

THE LOWER ABDOMEN

Kicking power originates from the lower abdomen, also called the danjun or dantien. A sharp exhalation during the execution of each kick tenses the abdomen, increasing the power of the kick. Many martial artists combine this exhalation with a shout (called kihap or kiai).

THE ARMS

For kicking, your arms aid in balance, acceleration and delivery of force. Because your arms can move freely on the horizontal, vertical or diagonal planes, they are excellent tools for counter-balancing the movement of your legs, particularly when learning a new kick. For example, when you learn the axe kick, sharply dropping your arms at your sides can help you raise your kicking leg higher.

THE LEGS

The legs are the primary impact delivery tools for kicking, however they must work in concert with the rest of the body for optimum power, speed and flexibility. Kicking only with your legs will produce poor results and limit your potential for improvement. As you saw in Chapter 1, your legs are the transmitters of the power that originates in your hips and torso.

The legs also support and disperse the body's weight. The knees in particular function to generate force in moving, lifting, and striking and to lessen the impact when landing or falling.

BALANCE POINT

NTEGRATED MOVEMENT

racticing kicking alone is not sufficient improve your kicking skills. Be sure to clude strength, timing, accuracy, balnce, power and flexibility exercises in our workout sessions to develop your verall physical condition. By taking a hole body approach, your physical ovements will become integrated and our confidence will increase.

t right are some sample exercises:
. Plyometric jumping drills, 2. Resistance band training (upper body),
. Core strengthening bodyweight xercises, 4. Resistance band training ower body), 5. Anti-gravity exercises,
. Dynamic isometric drills.*

*For more details, see *Ultimate Fitness Through Martial Arts* and *Ultimate Flexibility*

Every kick has a different balance angle:

Knee kick: forward hunch balances upraised knee

Axe kick: similar to knee kick balance

✳ BALANCE POINT

BALANCE:
IT'S ABOUT RELATIONSHIPS

BALANCE IN KICKING requires an understanding of where the various parts of your body are located in relation to each other; where they are moving from and to; and how to orchestrate them to maintain your form throughout a kick.

THE KEY to this seemingly complex process is maintaining symmetry in your body, if not visually, then at least in terms of weight distribution.

FOR EXAMPLE, **knee kick** requires you to slightly hunch your upper body forward to balance the upraised knee. The same is true of **axe kick**. Because **front kick** travels more forward than upward, your upper body needs to decline slightly backward to balance the forward motion of your leg. **Roundhouse kick** and **side kick** require a similar decline of the upper body to balance the outstretched leg.

Front kick: slight upper body decline

Roundhouse kick: upper body declines in relation to upraised kicking leg

Side kick: upper body declines in relation to thrusting height of kicking leg

BALANCE IS ABOUT CENTERING

In any balancing activity, the most important thing is to center yourself. Relax your shoulders and arms to promote natural rhythm in your motions. Lower your center of gravity so that you feel comfortable and secure. Do not overextend your body.

EXERCISE: When you practice spinning kicks like those shown below, tense your lower abdomen to focus your center and relax your terminals (upper body and kicking leg). When you feel confident with a spinning kick, try practicing 2, 3, 4 or 5 in quick succession with the same leg to see how this affects your balance. If your kick is technically, you should have no problem.

After kicking, let go until the force becomes zero, then let your leg return to its natural original position.

Keep your torso balanced between both legs for high kicks.

THE BONES

KEY POINT:
Kicking requires coordination of complex movements of the legs, hips, spine, shoulders, arms and head. The bones of your skeleton facilitate these movements.

OVERVIEW:
The skeletal structure of the body protects the organs and provides levers to facilitate movement. The placement of each bone is deliberate, exact, and in many cases, symmetrical. These characteristics are important to kicking because your kicking needs to be deliberate, precise and balanced. The symmetrical structure of the skeletal system enables us to balance our body by stabilizing it against gravity.

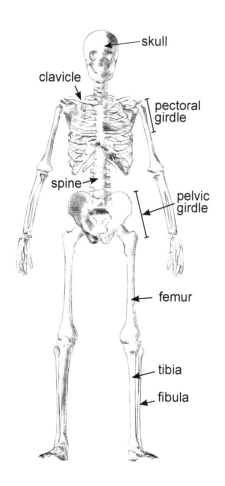

Additionally understanding the anti-gravitational nature of the spine, pelvic girdle and the lower limbs is critical since we must stand and kick in opposition gravity and often we must struggle enormously against an opponent. For standing kicks, for instance, you need to stabilize your standing leg and spine to free the kicking leg from the constraint of gravity (photo a). For jumping kicks, extend both legs when the spine reaches the highest point of the jump where gravity is weakest (photo b).

Photo a: standing front kick

Another key point to understand about the skeleton is that it made up of bones of varying lengths and functions. For example, the femur, the most powerful bone in the human body, allows us to control the speed and power of a kick.

The tiny phalanges, or toe bones, play almost no role in creating powerful kicks but they are critical in maintaining your balance while standing on one leg. Without toes, you would no more be able to deliver a proper roundhouse kick than if you lacked a femur bone. Each bone is designed to play a particular role in movement.

The skeleton by itself, however, is useless. It can only function with the help of the muscles and nervous system.

Photo b: jumping split kick

MAJOR BONES

SKULL

The skull is made up of 29 bones forming the brain case and face. For kicking, it is important to know the the jawbone is the only moving bone in the skull. Tuck your chin and close your mouth when kicking.

SPINE

The spine is attached to the pectoral girdle at the shoulder, the pelvic girdle at the hip, and the rib cage (12 ribs on each side) at the torso, giving shape and height to the body for support. The vertebrae of the spine are made up of alternating layers of bone and compressible cartilage, which reduces shock, bears the weight of the body and prevents the vertebrae from grinding against each other.

PECTORAL GIRDLE

The pectoral girdle is the set of bones that connect the arms with the shoulders. It is composed of the clavicle and scapular.

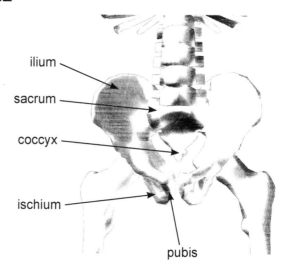

ARM

There are 30 bones in the arm, 27 of them in the hands and wrist. The arms are balance equalizers, initiators and accelerators in kicking.

PELVIC GIRDLE

The pelvic girdle is located at the bottom of the spine. It consists of the sacrum, coccyx, and a pair of hip bones (ilium, ischium, and pubis). The pelvic girdle is the source of power in kicking.

LEG

There are 30 bones in the leg, 22 of them in the ankle and foot. The femur, the most powerful and largest bone in human body, can bear a tremendous amount of pressure and weight. It is engineered for maximum strength and power. As a whole, the leg bones function to resist gravity by bearing the weight of the body during motion and at rest.

SPINAL CURVE

The spine is the backbone of the body: not only carrying the weight but also facilitating movement through mechanical balancing and counterbalancing. The 4 alternating curves in the spine aid in this job.

As you can see in the illustration at right, the spine is not a straight rod, but a flexible series of slight curves.

In kicking, the lumbar curve (1) and sacral curve (2) are the initiators of movement. The thoracic curve (3) and cervical curve (4) are the counterbalancing points.

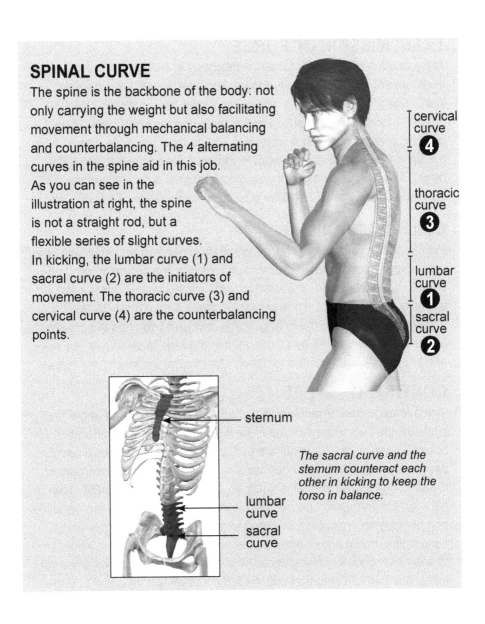

cervical curve
4

thoracic curve
3

lumbar curve
1

sacral curve
2

sternum

lumbar curve

sacral curve

The sacral curve and the sternum counteract each other in kicking to keep the torso in balance.

THE JOINTS

A joint is a point where two or more bones are connected. Although each joint works differently according to how the bones are joined, they are all built for movement and function as mechanical fulcrums. Therefore they play invaluable roles in kicking: transmission of force, facilitation of coiling/uncoiling the body and control of speed.

TRANSMISSION OF FORCE

The joints are responsible for chain reactions in kicking: force originates from one source (for example, the left shoulder for right roundhouse kick), activating the motion of the pelvic girdle, travels through the limb (right leg for right roundhouse kick) to the extremity (right foot). To visualize this, imagine cracking a whip. You initiate the force in your hand and the force travels through the whip to the opposite end, which strikes a target. The whip is a powerful weapon because it is an efficient transmitter of force. (See page 22-23 for a detailed explanation of this concept.)

COILING/UNCOILING

For circular techniques like roundhouse kick, turn kick and spinning whip kick, when a joint pivots in preparation for kicking, a coiling of force occurs. In the execution of the kick, an uncoiling action delivers the force of the kick to the target. For example, in steps 4-7 on page 35, the hip and knee joints create the coiling action and your body has the greatest amount of potential energy at this point in the kick. In steps 8-9, the knee and hip joints have uncoiled to deliver the force of the kick to the target.

CONTROL OF SPEED

When force passes through a joint, according to the pivoting angle and intensity, the joint magnifies the force which results in an acceleration of speed. However, if your joints are stiff, your speed will decrease as force passes through them. To understand why, think back to the example of the whip. When you crack the whip, your action has one point of initiation—your hand—and one point of final force transmission—the opposite end of the whip. Imagine if you tried to control the whip not only at the handle end, but at two or three points in the middle. The force would be chaotic and randomly dispersed. The same is true of your kick when your joints lack the fluidity to transmit the force smoothly from origin to target.

SEQUENCE OF KICKING

Action #1: The contraction of the abdomen muscles pulls the lumbar curve forward (1).

Action #2: Action #1 triggers the sacral curve to snap froward (2).

Action #3: Action #2 causes the sternum and neck (3) to counterbalance the forward motion of the hip. Actions #1-3 take place almost simultaneously, in a fraction of a second.

Action #4: The left shoulder begins to turn to the left.

Action #5: The right hip joint projects forward.

Action #6: As the right hip begins to rotate to the forward left, the elbows (6) move to the right to counterbalance.

Action #7: As the elbows swing to the right, the right knee moves to the left in a circular motion.

Action #8: As the right knee reaches the high point, both hands snap further to the right, accelerating the force of the leg.

Action #9: The right foot impacts the target at maximum speed and power.

repose   8-9   4-7   1-3   ready

✳ BALANCE POINT

WHAT IS BALANCE?

Balance is the ability to maintain your body position both in movement and at rest. There are two types of balance: static and dynamic. **Static balance** is a stationary object at equilibrium, like when you stand upright. **Dynamic balance**, a.k.a. balance in motion, is a body moving at constant linear and angular velocities.

WHERE DOES IT COME FROM?

1. Balance at rest and in motion both originate with good **posture**. Align your feet, hips, spine and head when kicking to maintain a stable upright posture.

2. Keep your eyes fixed on one spot, preferably your target. **Vision** provides your body with a ready means of finding your position relative to the ground through the presence or absence of visual cues.

3. **Tactile cues**, such as the network of sensors in the pads of your feet, relay important information to your brain, allowing it to adjust your weight distribution and foot position as necessary.

4. The **vestibular apparatus** in the inner ear controls the righting reflex which helps you remain upright in motion.

<u>KEY POINT</u>: If your lose your balance, restore it quickly by first positioning your head upright and fixing your line of sight on one object, then allow your body to follow.

THE MUSCLES

PRIMARY FUNCTION

The primary function of the muscles is to create movement of the skeleton (bones) through contraction and relaxation. Strengthening your major kicking muscles will enhance the power and flexibility of your kicks and help prevent common injuries.

MAJOR KICKING MUSCLES

For fast, powerful, well-controlled kicks, you need to develop three major muscle groups in the body:

- **abdominal muscles**: rectus and transversus abdominis muscles, oblique muscles
- **frontal thigh muscles**: quadriceps femoris
- **rear leg muscles**: gluteus muscles in the buttock, hamstring

The abdominal and thigh muscles produce power for front kick, roundhouse kick, axe kick and side kick. The rear leg muscles generate force for back kick, whip kick and spin whip kick as well as jumping kicks.

DEVELOPING ABDOMINAL MUSCLES

The best exercises to develop strong abdominal muscles are sit-ups, including side and twisting sit-ups, crunches, V-ups, knee raises, leg raises, side leg raises and hanging leg raises.* Use a wide variety of exercises to be sure you are working the lower, mid, upper and oblique ab muscles. And don't forget to include back strengthening exercises in your workout to develop a well-balanced torso musculature.

DEVELOPING LEG MUSCLES

The best exercises to develop strong thigh and buttocks muscles are standing jumps, squats (with or without weight), lunges, sprinting, bounding, stair running and hill running.* Be sure to stretch at every workout so that your leg muscles do not become overly tight from strength training.

---

* For more information on the above exercises, see *Ultimate Fitness Through Martial Arts*, Sang H. Kim, Turtle Press.

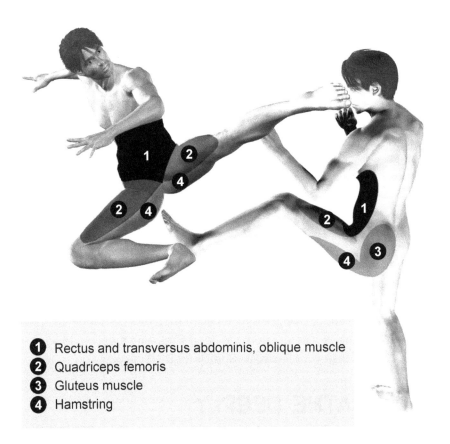

1. Rectus and transversus abdominis, oblique muscle
2. Quadriceps femoris
3. Gluteus muscle
4. Hamstring

SAMPLE KICK STRENGTHENING WORKOUT*

Lunges, 10 reps, 1-3 sets
Squats, 10 reps, 1-3 sets
Crunches, 10 reps, 1-3 sets
Side sit-ups, 10 reps, 1-3 sets
V-ups, 5 reps, 1-3 sets
Alternating knee raise, 5 reps, 1-3 sets
Alternating leg raise, 5 reps, 1-3 sets
Double leg raise, 5 reps, 1-3 sets
Bench leg raise, 5 reps, 1-3 sets

50 yard sprint, 3 reps
50 yard uphill run, 3 reps
25 yard bounding, 3 reps
Stair run, 1 flight, 3 reps

BEFORE KICKING...

1. WARM UP

Warm up before engaging in full-speed kicking to raise your body temperature and increase circulation. A good warm up enhances the ability of the muscles to contract and warm muscles stretch better. Begin with easy gross motor activities, gradually increasing in intensity from mild to vigorous. Control your movements while loading calculated stress on the muscles. Warm up for 15 minutes.

2. STRETCH

Before practice, always stretch your muscles to prepare them for the demands of kicking. Stretching increases the elasticity of the muscles, which enables you to have a greater range of motion and strength, and thus increases your capacity to generate more power. Stretching before kicking practice should include simple, dynamic exercises (see examples on page 41). This is different from the deep stretching that you do after practice to increase your flexibility. Stretch for 5-10 minutes.

3. BREATHE DEEPLY

Deep breathing relaxes the muscles by providing ample oxygen to the cells. Deep belly breathing also enhances posture, circulation, relaxation and inner power. Consequently the mind becomes clear and the body works more efficiently. Deep breathing before practice eliminates the distractions of the body and mind and promotes mind-body unity. Breathe deeply for 3-5 minutes.

4. VISUALIZE

Visualization is active mental imagery to create familiarity with a specific target movement. For example, close your eyes and think of the beginning, middle and end of a side kick. Look closely at critical points such as pivoting your hip before impact. Replay it over and over until you get it right in your mind. Finally complete the entire sequence with a smooth and perfectly timed performance. Visualize one technique for 3-5 minutes.

WARM-UP OPTIONS
Jumping jacks x 100
Push-ups x 50
Sit-ups x 100
Jump rope x 3 mins.
Running x 15 mins.

DYNAMIC LEG RAISES
Hold the bar and raise your
knee 10 times on each
side, then swing your leg
up, smoothly with control,
10 times on each side. This
exercise develops kick-
ing posture, precision and
strength while warming up
the kicking muscles.

LEG RAISE & HOLD
Hold the bar and raise your
leg in a controlled kicking
motion (left: whip kick, right:
back kick) as high as you
can and hold it for as long as
you can. This will stretch and
strengthen your leg muscles
and develop balance and
posture simultaneously.

STRETCHING
There are two types of
stretching: stretching as
part of your warm-up, which
is brief and dynamic, and
stretching to develop flexibility (below), which is done
after practice and can take
up to 30 minutes.

KNOCKOUT POINTS

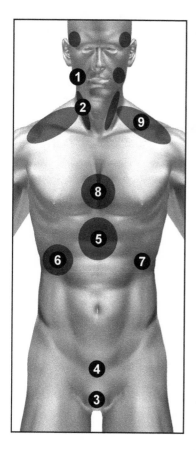

A knockout kick renders your opponent unconsciou by either stopping the sup-ply of oxygen and blood to the brain, causing insuf-ferable pain or causing a shock to the brain.

MAJOR KNOCKOUT POINTS

1. Head: Kicks to the head can shock the brain and shut down the function of the nervous system. A kick to the jaw for instance causes a rebounding effect in the brain, momentarily nullifying the function of the nervous system, which renders the opponent unconscious.

2. Neck (Carotid Artery): Striking the carotid sinus can lead to a sudden drop in blood pressure and heart rate which can cause a loss of consciousness and, in some cases, death. Because striking the carotid sinus relies simply on triggering a physiological reaction, even a ligh strike can result in a knockout. Striking the neck is illega in most combat sports.

3. Groin and 4. Pelvic Plexus: These targets are also generally not legal in combat sports, but are effective knockout targets for self-defense because they can be hit with a powerful low section kick.

5. Solar Plexus and 8. Cardiac Plexus: These two targets have to be struck with great force with a powerfu kick like a side kick, to achieve a knockout. Kicking this area can also "knock the wind out of" an opponent.

6. Liver and 7. Kidneys (both sides): These three targets can be easily struck with roundhouse kick. Even if you don't achieve a knockout, kicks to the liver or kid-neys will weaken an opponent's stamina and will.

9. Brachial Plexus: This target is vulnerable to an axe kick. If the plexus strike does not cause a knockout, it can result in serious damage to the clavicle bone.

FUNDAMENTAL
KICKS

Kicking is one of the most fun and natural activities in the martial arts. This chapter has 12 fundamental kicks and for each kick you'll find the purpose of the kick, key points to pay attention to, common targets, how-to, variations, applications specific to self-defense, traditional martial arts practice and combat sports, common mistakes and practice drills.

blade front kick

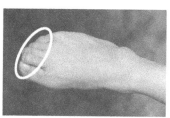

toes

instep

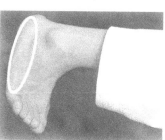

blade

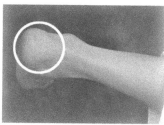

rear heel

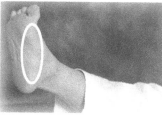

arch

KICKING WEAPONS

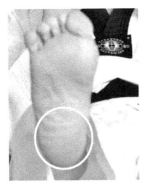

bottom heel

ball

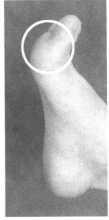

side of ball

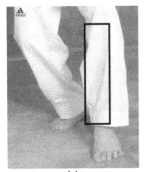

shin

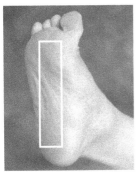

sole

knee

PURPOSE

Front kick is used to strike a target that is directly in front of you. If your opponent is on your side or rear, simply turn your body in that direction and kick. Front kick is the most direct way to knock down an opponent by kicking the groin, face or neck. You can also use it to deter an advancing opponent by attacking the kneecap, shin or thigh.

KEY POINTS

Bend your kicking knee acutely and snap the ball or instep of your foot quickly and powerfully to the target. If you are wearing shoes, kick with the toe or instep of your shoe. In a self-defense situation, aim for the middle of the body or leg to increase your chances of striking the target.

STRIKING AREA

Ball, instep, toes, bottom of the foot

TARGETS

1. groin
2. lower abdomen
3. solar plexus
4. chest
5. neck
6. mouth
7. frontal thigh
8. kneecap
9. shin

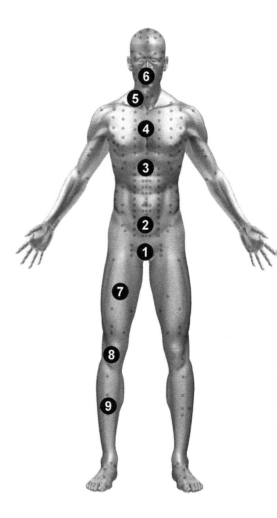

HOW TO

1. From fighting stance, shift your weight to the front leg.

2. Bring your knee up, pointing it at the target.

3. As your hip snaps forward, extend your knee and kick. Keep your standing knee bent, using the thigh muscles to firmly stabilize your stance. Tuck your chin down, lean your torso slightly backward to add extra reach (length). Exception: If you are moving forward, bring your torso forward instead of leaning back.

4. Withdraw the foot quickly after the kick and repose.

FRONT VIEW of front kick: notice the position of the left hand to protect the groin and the right hand to maintain balance. You can also keep your hands up in a guard position. The head, hip and standing foot are aligned vertically for maximum stability.

SPORT APPLICATION: Front kick to the neck using the blade of the foot. (Kicking the neck is not allowed in some combat sports.)

APPLICATIONS

Front kick is the most direct and easiest kick to execute, so you can instinctively throw it in almost any situation. For self-defense, it is useful for striking the groin, stomach or solar plexus directly, or in combination with a hold or lock. For sport competition, you can stop an opponent by kicking his lower abdomen or knock him down by kicking his neck vertically with the blade of your foot.

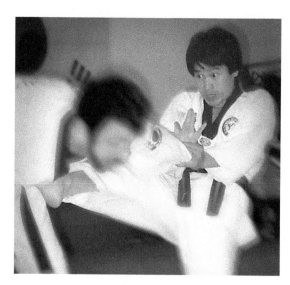

SELF-DEFENSE APPLICATION: Front kick to the chest in combination with a twisting wrist lock

SPORT APPLICATION: If an opponent rushes toward you, throw a front kick to push him away. As the opponent backs up, throw another front kick or a roundhouse kick or axe kick.

SELF-DEFENSE APPLICATION:
A front kick to the pelvic plexus can knock an opponent down. Push deeply into the pelvis with the ball or bottom of the foot.

SPORT APPLICATION:
Blade front kick to the carotid artery in the neck can result in a knock down or knockout. Recommended for advanced students only.

SELF-DEFENSE APPLICATION:
For front kick to the groin, use the full instep of the foot to drive upward.

COMMON MISTAKES

MISTAKE 1: The most serious mistake people make in executing a front kick is tilting the head, which disrupts your balance.
SOLUTION: Tuck your chin down toward your chest.

MISTAKE 2: Arm position: too wide, too narrow or too low.
SOLUTION: To practice keeping your arms close to your body in fighting stance, hold the collars of your uniform and practice.

MISTAKE 3: Excessively raising the heel of the standing foot.
SOLUTION: If you feel that you have to raise up onto the toes of your standing foot, pivot your standing foot slightly more when you kick or lower the height of your kick.

MISTAKE 4: Leaning too far back/away from the target.
SOLUTION: To kick, you should decline your torso slightly but not so much that you lose your balance. If you are leaning back too much, lower the height of your kick until you improve your flexibility or raise your knee higher when you chamber your kicking leg.

• REMEMBER

1. Keep your head straight.
2. Tuck your chin down.
3. Position both elbows at equal height.
4. Aim your knee at the target and kick directly to the target.

• AVOID

1. Tilting your head (**a**)
2. Leaning your torso too far backward
3. Opening your arms too wide
4. Dropping your hands
5. Holding your arms too tight in front of your chest
6. Lifting your standing heel excessively (**b**)

ROUNDHOUSE KICK

PURPOSE

Roundhouse kick is used to strike lateral targets on the trunk, head and legs of an opponent who is facing you. If your opponent stands sideways in front of you, kick the front of his torso. Due to its effectiveness and simplicity, roundhouse kick is the most commonly used kick in competition. It is a versatile weapon for attacking and counterattacking against any type of opponent.

KEY POINTS

Bend your kicking knee forward acutely, rotate your hip and snap the ball or instep of your foot quickly and powerfully to the target. When attacking, bring your body forward for more power. For counterattacking, turn your body sideways or lean slightly backward to avoid being hit.

STRIKING AREA

Ball, instep, shin, toes

TARGETS

1. rib cage
2. thigh (inside, outside)
3. knee (inside, outside)
4. ankle (inside, outside)
5. neck
6. head
7. chest
8. solar plexus
9. lower abdomen

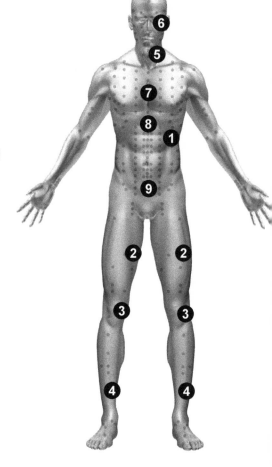

HOW TO

1. From fighting stance, shift your weight to the front leg.
2. Bring your knee up, pointing at the target as in front kick.
3. Pivot your standing foot and rotate your knee perpendicular to the target, while your arms move in the opposite direction to maintain your balance.
4. Rotate your hip into the kick until it is parallel to the target surface. Snap your foot out at the target. At impact, your entire body should be on the same plane. Keep your head up and look at the target.
5. Withdraw the foot quickly along the same path after the kick and repose.

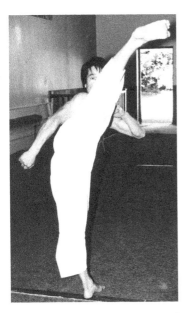

Roundhouse kick with the ball of
the foot

FRONT VIEW: *roundhouse
kick with the instep*

APPLICATIONS

Roundhouse kick is the most versatile kick for both competition and self-defense. For competition, it is safe, effective and powerful for striking low, middle, and high targets. For self-defense, it is useful for striking the knee, groin, and stomach. It is most effective when used in combination with punches, elbow strikes and knee kicks.

SPORT APPLICATIONS

When your opponent steps in to attack, use an intercepting roundhouse kick to stop him and score.

For high roundhouse kick, raise your knee high and shoot it quickly at the opponent's head.

Top: When your opponent throws a high section roundhouse kick, counter with a middle section roundhouse kick.

Right: When your opponent is retreating, step in and chase him with a roundhouse kick.

Below: If your opponent hesitates while attacking, throw a middle section intercepting roundhouse kick.

SPORT APPLICATION: *Kick as your opponent steps in to attack.*

MARTIAL ART APPLICATION: *Roundhouse kick in one step sparring*

SELF-DEFENSE APPLICATION: *Kick over the opponent's strike, using your longer range kick to your advantage.*

SELF-DEFENSE APPLICATION: *From the ground, use the ball of your foot to strike the opponent's chest. Place your hands on the ground to support your body and add power.*

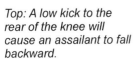

SELF-DEFENSE APPLICATIONS

Top: A low kick to the rear of the knee will cause an assailant to fall backward.

Right: On the ground, you can use a downward roundhouse kick to a fallen opponent.

Below: Maintain distance from your opponent on the ground with a roundhouse kick to the head.

COMMON MISTAKES

MISTAKE 1: The most common mistake when executing roundhouse kick is incomplete rotation of the hip.

SOLUTION: For maximum power, rotate your body fully to align your hip, head and feet, and to put your bodyweight into your kick.

MISTAKE 2: Over-rotation of the body during and after kicking.

SOLUTION: It can be easy to over-rotate your body in an effort to make your kick more powerful, but power comes from speed and the snap of your hips, not from turning your upper body, so focus on these instead.

MISTAKE 3: Kicking in a wide arc.

SOLUTION: Bring your knee up straight at the target and then pivot tightly. Avoid letting your leg swing wide; instead snap it at the target.

BOTTOM LINE: Keep your opponent in sight at all times; kick fast and forcefully; repose as quickly as you can.

• REMEMBER

1. Keep your head straight.
2. Tuck your chin down.
3. Rotate your hip fully.
4. Move your arms naturally around your body for balance and power.

1. A risky uncommitted kick leaves the kicker (R) open to a counterattack.

2. A vulnerable, premature kick falls short of the opponent.

• AVOID

1. Uncommitted kicking
2. Premature kicking (bad timing)
3. Tilting your head
4. Over-rotating your body
5. Kicking in a wide arc
6. Kicking at the wrong distance (too close to opponent **a**)

ROUNDHOUSE KICK FORM DRILL

To improve your kicking, practice roundhouse kick holding a support. Start with your back to the wall and your kicking foot in the rear. Pivot so your hip faces the wall and your chest is parallel to the wall. Standing close to the wall will prevent your from over-rotating your hips or knees and from hunching your upper body forward. Finally, extend your kicking leg and hold briefly. Your body (chest, hips, kicking leg) should be parallel to the wall when your kick is fully extended.

ROUNDHOUSE KICK POWER DRILL

The heavy bag is an excellent tool for developing power. Here are examples of heavy bag kicking drills: 1) 3 sets of 15 kicks with each leg at normal power and speed. 2) Be sure you're fully warmed up, then kick as high as you can 20 times on each side. 3) Kick as fast and as powerfully as you can to a middle level target, alternating legs for 50 kicks on each side.

ROUNDHOUSE KICK PRECISION DRILL

Ideally, you should develop precision from the start of the learning process. A good way to do this is to always have a specific target for each kick. You can use a hand target held by a partner, a ball suspended on a string or a heavy bag. When you practice with the heavy bag, mark it with tape as shown here so you do not fall into the habit of randomly kicking the bag. Whether you are training for precision with slow controlled kicks or you are working on power and speed, stay disciplined and try to hit your target every time.

PURPOSE

Side kick is a powerful kick that transmits the weight of your entire body into the target. It is an effective weapon to stop an incoming opponent by pushing his knee joint or kicking his stomach. It is also useful as an initiative attack to push an opponent backward and then throw a powerful follow-up kick.

KEY POINTS

Pivot your body and chamber your knee so that your kicking leg is perpendicular to the vertical target line before kicking. Pivoting and alignment of your hips, legs and shoulders are paramount.

STRIKING AREA

Blade, bottom of the heel, bottom of the foot

TARGETS

1. knee
2. thigh
3. pelvic crease
4. shin
5. ankle
6. rib cage
7. stomach
8. armpit
9. neck

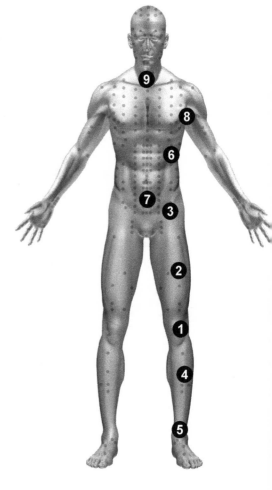

HOW TO

1. From fighting stance, shift your weight to the front leg.
2. Bring your knee up, pointing at the target.
3. Pivot your standing foot so your body is oriented laterally to the target. Be sure to fully pivot your hip so that your kicking foot, buttock, shoulder and head are aligned.
4. Snap your knee and shoot the blade of your foot into the target. Align your toes lower than your heel for maximum power. Keep your head up and your head, shoulder, hip, knee and foot on one plane.
5. Withdraw the foot quickly after the kick and repose.

FRONT VIEW of side kick: notice the kicking foot, hip, standing foot, shoulder and head are aligned and the arms cover the chest and lower torso.

VARIATIONS

You can use side kick to hit any target: low, middle or high, standing or on the ground. The key is to kick quickly, but to align your body correctly no matter what the situation and penetrate the target deeply with your kicking foot. In a self-defense situation, it's acceptable and even helpful to place one or both hands on the ground for support and added power.

High side kick with the right arm stretched out along with the kicking leg for balance

✳ BALANCE POINT

High side kick has 3 key elements: 1. a strong support leg; 2. a flexible kicking leg; 3. strong ab muscles to stabilize the torso. To kick at your maximum height, for demonstration purposes or to test yourself, it helps to drop your torso (as shown here) while keeping your eye on the target.

Top: High side kick with support

Right: Modified angular side kick

Below: Upward side kick on ground

APPLICATIONS

The side kick is popular for self-defense and board breaking demonstrations for its dynamic and aesthetic impression. But far more impressive than the look of a crisp high side kick is its destructive capacity in self-defense and fighting. With good timing and distance, one perfectly executed side kick can knock an opponent out of the ring or to his knees.

SPORT APPLICATIONS

Above left: A high side kick is a good counterattack when an opponent steps in to attack.

Above right: A middle section side kick is a good way to push an opponent backward to create additional distance in sparring.

Left: Using the heel of your foot to kick to the face of an unguarded opponent can result in a knockout.

Top: Side kick demonstration

SELF-DEFENSE APPLICATIONS:
*Right top: When an opponent
lunges toward you, kick the inside of
his knee to stop his advance.*

*Right: A side kick to the rear of the
opponent's lead leg is a quick and
easy way to knock him to his knees.*

☘ *BALANCE POINT*

SIDE KICK: TOES UP OR DOWN?

For maximum power, your toes should be lower than your heel when you perform a side kick. This creates a slight downward turn to your kicking foot and drives your heel into the target. It also aligns your body weight directly behind your kick and aids in balance. If your foot is not turned slightly downward on impact, you might be unbalanced backward by a stronger opponent or an opponent who resists by throwing his weight forward into you. It is easier to turn your foot downward when you completely rotate your hips.

Top: When you catch or trap an opponent's kicking leg,
throw a low side kick to the upper calf to take him down.

Below: Use the long reach of the side kick to ward off an
opponent with a weapon.

Top: If you've fallen or been thrown to the ground, quickly throw a side kick into the rear of the assailant's knee to knock him down and away from you.

Bellow: Side kick can also be used when both fighters are on the ground.

COMMON MISTAKES

MISTAKE 1: Curved body or hip sticking out to the rear.
SOLUTION: The key to power in the side kick lies in precise body alignment. Don't let your hip leave the force line of the kick. Stretch your body fully so that your torso, hip, knee and foot are aligned on the same plane.

MISTAKE 2: Dropping the head.
SOLUTION: Look at the target over your kicking side shoulder.

MISTAKE 3: Kicking too high.
SOLUTION: For practical applications, side kick should be powerful and a kick that's too high can lack power because your body is no longer behind the kick. Choose a realistic target height.

• REMEMBER

1. Align your hip, knee, and foot, and kick along the shortest path to the target.
2. Rotate your hip fully for power.
3. Strike the target with the blade or bottom of the foot.
4. Lower the toes slightly below the heel to enhance power and balance.

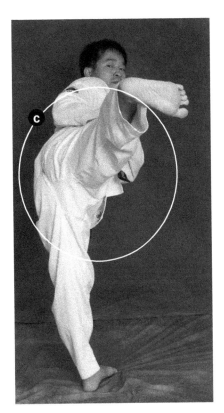

• AVOID

1. Dropping your head or taking your eye off the target (**a**)
2. Kicking too high for the situation (**b**)
3. Curved body alignment, hip sticking out to the rear (**c**)

ONE THOUGHT ONE ACTION DRILL

Although every technique has multiple stages of execution, you should do each kick as a single action without separation in time and motion. In the beginning, this will be very hard; it might even seem impossible. But there are many exercises and drills you can use to develop muscle memory and reach the single action stage: visualization, kicking at the stretching bar, practicing with a handheld or suspended target, doing timed target kicking drills (how long does 5 kicks take? 10?), shadow sparring and incorporating kicks into sparring, self-defense or forms practice routines. Finally, ultimately, try to skip the thought process of bringing your knee up, rotating the body to the side, looking at the target, etc. Just kick. Fast.

Left: Hold the stretching bar and visualize the motion of side kick before you kick.

Below: Kick, internalize the process, and adjust your posture. Repeat at least 50 times a day on each side to develop muscle memory for every new kick you learn.

✱ BALANCE POINT

FOR A GREAT KICK:

1. Learn, understand and internalize the mechanics of the technique.

2. Aim at a target of a reasonable height and distance.

3. Kick fast. A fast kick provides you with less time to think and analyze, so your body naturally adjusts and controls itself.

PENETRATING FORCE

Kicking power comes from the combination of your body weight, the speed of the kick, and the distance covered. Since your body weight is constant, it is important to increase your kicking speed and to release your kick into the target to the fullest extent possible. Think of kicking several inches behind the target, into the center of the heavy bag or behind your opponent's body. Strive for penetrating force, not pushing force, by releasing the full weight of your body into the target at impact.

Right: Aim for a target that is several inches behind the one you want to strike and stretch your kick to the fullest.

Below: Explosive penetrating force causes the target to collapse rather than be pushed away. Imagine the effect on a human torso.

✱ BALANCE POINT

TIPS FOR HIGH SIDE KICK:

You should be practical with side kick; generally, you do not need to kick higher than stomach level. However, if you want to improve the height of your side kick, here are some exercises you can do:

1) Do low horse riding stance for 60 seconds (photo 2). Rest for 30 seconds.

2) Do a deeper horse riding stance for 60 seconds.

3) Squat down and hold your ankles. Breathe deeply for 60 seconds.

4) From step #3, put both hands on the floor in front of you. Slide your right foot all the way to the right and stretch your right leg for 60 seconds. Repeat with the left leg.

5) Stand up and walk around while breathing deeply and shaking your legs and ankles to loosen up the muscles and joints.

6) Hold a bar, chair or table for support, and raise your right leg for a slow side kick. Hold in the air as long as you can. Repeat on the left side. Do a minimum of 3 sets of 15 seconds on both sides.

7) If your have a partner, let him hold your leg and raise it slowly in side position to a little past the point where you are comfortable. If you don't have a partner, you can use a wall (photo 3) to support your kick. Repeat 3 times on each side, holding for 15 seconds each. Eventually you might be able to use a door frame for this exercise (photo 1)

Repeat steps #1-7 three times a week for twelve weeks. Monitor your progress weekly by keeping a journal so you can see your progress over the three month period. It is important to know your limits and progress from there. As long as you are making positive progress, where you began from isn't very important.

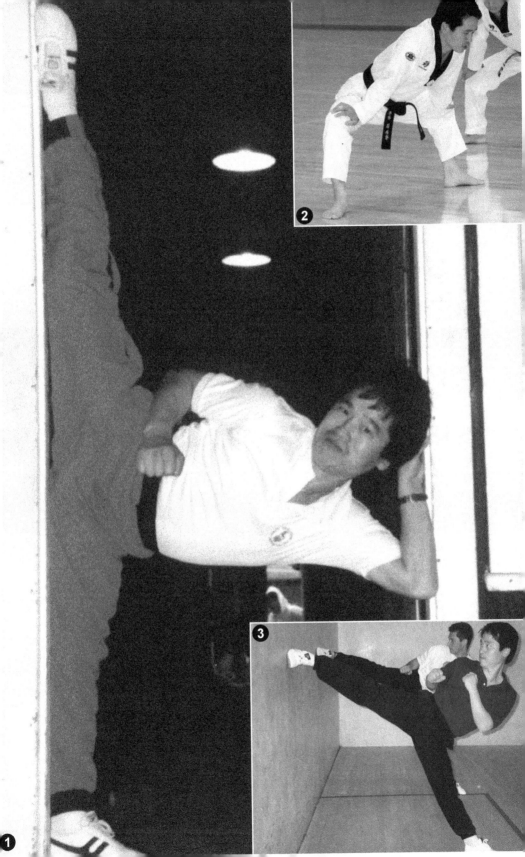

PURPOSE

Knee kick is used to strike an opponent in close quarters or ground fighting. The main goal of knee kicking is to systematically drain the opponent's energy and will by inflicting pain on exposed targets like the thigh, rib cage, stomach and groin. For advanced practitioners, a jumping knee kick to the head can be a deadly weapon.

KEY POINTS

Secure the opponent by holding his neck, head or torso before kicking. Precisely attack vital points such as the groin, outer thigh, and rib cage.

STRIKING AREA

Upper knee, frontal knee, inner knee

TARGETS

1. groin
2. lower abdomen
3. solar plexus
4. sternum
5. head
6. rib cage
7. thigh (outside, inside)
8. knee

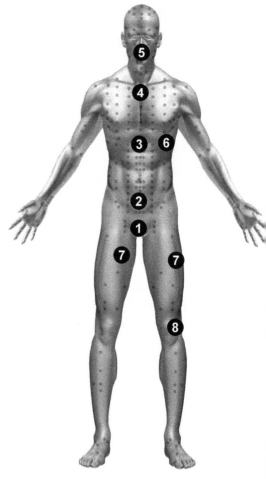

HOW TO

1. From fighting stance, shift your weight to the front leg.
2. Raise your knee toward the target.
3. Snap the pelvis and thrust the knee upward while pulling down with your hands and sharply exhaling as you tighten your abdomen muscles.
4. For repetitive knee strikes, set your foot down toward the rear of your stance. For combination strikes, set your foot down in front, close to the opponent.

BALANCE POINT

JMPING KNEE KICK

umping knee kick is one of the most
vanced fighting techniques. When you
liver a jumping knee kick, keep your
ad up, focus your attention on your
ver abdomen, and try to form a trian-
lar shape with your body (your striking
ee is the tip of the triangle). Notice how
mpact the body is at the moment of
pact (right).

FRONT VIEW: Begin practicing with
a mid-height knee kick. Hold this
position for 15 seconds at a time to
develop pelvic control.

VARIATIONS

Knee kicks vary from style to style and performer to performer. You can kick vertically, horizontally or diagonally, upward, downward, inward or outward. Or you can kick in some combination of the above. The knee kick is the most versatile kick, particularly in combat sports.

BOTTOMLINE: Strive to develop absolute pelvic control to manipulate the direction and force of the knee kick.

Left: Straight upward knee kick

Right: Roundhouse knee kick to the middle section

Left: Jumping roundhouse knee kick

Right: Jumping horizontal knee kick

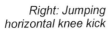

THE KNEE: THE KING OF KICKS

The knees are the most powerful weapon of your body. In most tradition-al martial arts competition, knee kicks are prohibited due to their poten-tially dangerous effects. In modern combat arts, knee kicks are known for their brutal destructive force in both standing and ground fighting.

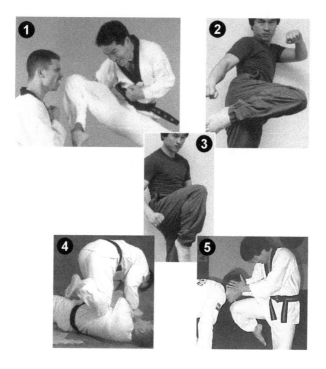

1. Straight jumping knee kick delivers the entire body weight with speed and the element of surprise. 2. Roundhouse knee kick is powered by the coiling force of the torso. 3. Front knee kick is aided by the hands pulling the target into the thrusting knee. 4. Horizontal knee kick on the ground is a good way to break an opponent's will to fight. 5. Holding or pulling the opponent's head down into the kick adds force and ensures an accurate strike.

Visualization Drill:
Visualize the target height
before you jump and close
the gap mentally as you
repeat the physical jumps.

TRAINING
TIPS

VISUALIZE YOUR KICK

There are two types of visualization that you can use
to improve your kicking. The more basic method is
technique-specific. Begin with this and then move on
to the mind-specific method as you advance.

1. Technique-specific: See or visualize yourself doing a technique step-by-step in great detail, such as
the five stages of each kick: Ready, Shift, Pivot, Kick,
and Repose. This is a good way to improve the accuracy of a technique.

2. Mind-specific: Mentally focus on the technique as
a whole. In your mind, see yourself giving a perfect
performance, like a movie star. This is a good way to
improve the speed and efficiency of your techniques.

APPLICATIONS

Knee kick is the most powerful kick in a close quarters fight. A solid knee kick to the outer thigh or groin can easily send an opponent to the floor. A kick to the rib cage or solar plexus can stop the opponent's breathing. A kick to the chin or the nose can result in an instant knockout. On the ground, a knee kick is useful for keeping an opponent on defense or weakening his resolve.

SPORT APPLICATIONS

Grasp the side or rear of the opponent's head to hold him in place for an upward knee kick.

Grab behind the opponent's neck to drive his body downward into your roundhouse knee kick to the lower abdomen.

**SELF-DEFENSE
APPLICATIONS**

A drop knee kick is a powerful way to finish a downed assailant.

Subdue a struggling assailant with knee kicks to the ribs.

COMMON MISTAKES

MISTAKE 1: The most common error in knee kicking is angle control - either because the knee is not folded tightly or because the hip is opened too wide.

SOLUTION: Keep your knee folded as sharply as possible and thrust your pointed knee using the snapping force of your pelvis. By keeping your knee folded tightly and using your pelvis to control the direction of the kick, you'll find it easier to control the angle of your strike.

MISTAKE 2: Another common problem is distance control, often due to hesitation.

SOLUTION: Don't wait for perfect time to strike. In practice, focus on seizing the moment and throwing your knee instinctively to openings on the thigh, stomach, kidney, chest, neck or head.

• REMEMBER

1. Point your knee.
2. Use your pelvis for power and control.
3. Practice short, middle, and long knee kicks.
4. Synchronize the upward motion of your knee with the downward movement of your hands.
5. Exhale when kicking.

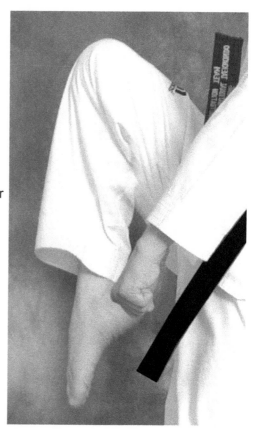

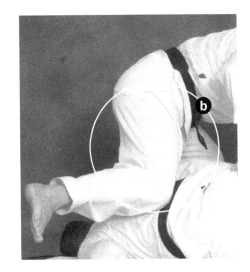

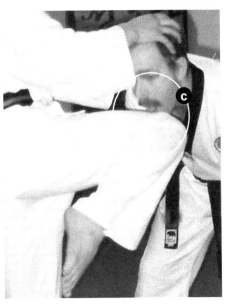

• AVOID

1. Poor angle of kick, not folding the knee tightly (**a**)
2. Wide arc of kick, opening your hip too wide (**b**)
3. Tardy execution
4. Muscle tension
5. Striking with the edge of the kneecap (**c**)
6. Self-injury

PURPOSE

Raising kick is used to improve leg flexibility. However, if you drop your foot with force after raising it, it becomes an axe kick. If you kick an opponent who is behind you, it becomes a rear kick. It can also scare an opponent into backing up so you can follow up with a primary kick.

KEY POINTS

Relax your body and keep your torso erect to gain kicking height. Keep your arms near the kicking leg for balance and control.

STRIKING AREA

Ball, toes, bottom of the foot, heel

TARGETS

1. head
2. sternum

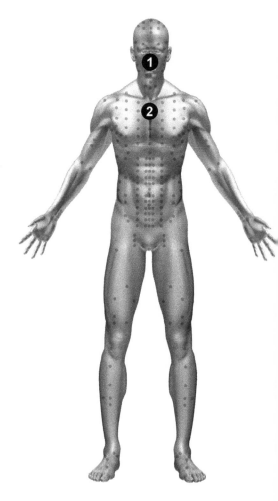

HOW TO

1. From fighting stance, shift your weight to the front leg.
2. Bring your straight leg up toward your chest and let your foot go over your shoulder. Do not put any power in this movement; simply focus on raising your leg as high as possible.
3. Return your leg along the same path in a relaxed but controlled way.

Breathe out as you raise your leg and breathe in as you lower your leg.

VARIATION

1. Pull your toes downward for an extra stretch in your hamstring muscles.

2. Point your toes to get extra length in your kick.

APPLICATIONS

Although raising kick is primarily used for improving flexibility and the height of your kicks, it can be practical in unusual ways, perhaps due to the element of surprise. In just the right situation, raising kick can be a practical way to shock an opponent with an unorthodox counter-movement.

SPORT APPLICATION

Use a quick, light raising kick to block an opponent's high front kick or inside crescent kick.

Above: Raising kick is a good way to improve your axe kick by dynamically stretching the hamstring muscles.

Right and above right: In this unorthodox self-defense application, you can throw a raising kick against an assailant who attacks from behind, striking with the the ball of the foot.

SELF-DEFENSE APPLICATION

COMMON MISTAKES

MISTAKE 1: Hunching the upper body.

SOLUTION: The most common cause of poor posture, especially in the torso, is excessive muscular tension, either because you are trying to kick too high or too hard. To remedy this, keep your upper body erect and relaxed while you raise your leg smoothly and without power.

MISTAKE 2: Raising up on the toes. This is also usually caused by kicking too high or too hard for your skill level and will often lead to another common mistake: lowering your upper body backwards.

SOLUTION: Relax and kick at an attainable height without power. Reduce muscle tension by having realistic expectations. Bend your standing leg (knee) slightly to eliminate the strain in your hamstrings that leads to raising up on your toes.

• REMEMBER

1. Keep your posture upright.
2. Relax your shoulders and neck.
3. Advance progressively.
4. Raise your leg smoothly, without power.
5. Exhale as you raise your leg.

Bending your standing knee slightly will allow you to kick higher while maintaining good posture. Keep your arms around your kicking leg for balance.

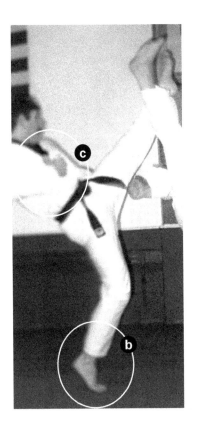

• AVOID

1. Struggling to kick higher than your present skill level allows
2. Trying to progress too quickly
3. Hunching your upper body (**a**)
4. Lifting your standing heel excessively (**b**)
5. Leaning your body backward (**c**)

TIMING & BREATHING

Breathing is key to converting internal energy to power. When your breathing and technique are in sync, your kick carries maximum force.

Breathe naturally as you move and your body will tell you when to breathe in and out. Here are some guidelines to help you get started:

1. For direct kicks, inhale before kicking and exhale when you kick. At the moment of impact, exhale sharply while tightening your lower belly.

2. For stepping kicks, inhale when you raise your leg, step forward, turn around, or jump. Exhale when you kick.

BOTTOMLINE: Power comes with exhalation at the moment of impact.

✴ BALANCE POINT

HOW TO KICK WELL
WITH YOUR WEAKER LEG:

1. Stretch the weaker leg muscles well and always warm up to prevent injuries.

2. Strengthen your weaker leg by doing very slow controlled kicks wearing a light (2 to 5 pound) ankle weight. Start with the lightest weight and work your way up. Start with 3 sets of 10 repetitions of front kick or roundhouse kick.

3. Remove the weight and do 10 repetitions slowly and then 10 more with speed.

4. Practice 3 sets of 15 repetitions on a heavy bag or handheld target with power.

5. Practice steps 1-4 consistently, 3 times per week. You should begin to see results in a few weeks. When you do, increase the number of sets, speed and power or try applying the exercises to more advanced kicks.

6. Track your progress in your training diary or notebook.

7. Re-evaluate your progress and revise your goals every two weeks.

OUTSIDE CRESCENT KICK

PURPOSE

Outside crescent kick is used to strike the opponent's face at an in-to-outward angle. It is similar to whip kick; the difference is that, for whip kick, you should turn your body fully to the side with a larger arc whereas for outside crescent kick, your body faces more to the front than the side.

KEY POINTS

From fighting stance, first rotate your upper body and coil your hip in the opposite direction of the target, then arc your foot in front of you, diagonally across the target.

STRIKING AREA

Blade, bottom or ball of the foot

TARGETS

1. face
2. neck

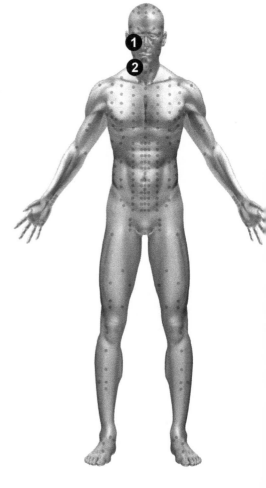

HOW TO

1. From fighting stance, shift your weight to the front leg and begin to rotate your front leg and torso diagonally away from the target.
2. Bring your foot above your head, arcing outward.
3. Snap your foot outward in an arc toward the target, striking the target at the top of the downturn.
4. After kicking, control your foot as you complete the outward arc and return to fighting stance. Maintain your center on your standing leg throughout the kick so your kicking leg is easier to control.

FOR STRONG FLEXIBLE KICKS

Kicks like crescent kick and axe kick derive their power from a large range of motion, so they require flexibility as much as muscular strength.

To develop power in these kicks, try using a bike tube or resistance band, with one end attached to a fixed object and the other to your ankle. Perform your kicks so that they are traveling away from the fixed end of the band, creating resistance for each repetition. Control your kicks to avoid injuring your joints during resistance training.

As you get stronger, add more tubing or heavier tubing to increase the resistance.

APPLICATIONS

Outside crescent kick is useful for kicking at or knocking away anything entering the vertical centerline of your body. You can kick an opponent's face or you can use your foot to deflect a punch, grab or kick. Outside crescent kick can strike a target with the bottom of the foot, the blade, the ankle, or even the shin.

* Begin with a low kick and kick higher as you get used to the motion.

Just after an opponent finishes an attack, counter with an outside crescent kick to the face using the bottom of the foot (timing and distance are the key factors).

SPORT APPLICATION

Top: Strike the assailant's knife wielding hand with the ankle of your outside crescent kick.

Below: Use the long range of the outside crescent kick to knock the opponent's punching hand away (attack while defending).

SELF-DEFENSE APPLICATIONS

* Outside crescent kick should be used with follow-up techniques such as:

Outside crescent kick + rear hand punch
Outside crescent kick + rear elbow strike
Outside crescent kick + rear leg front kick
Outside crescent kick + rear leg roundhouse kick
Outside crescent kick + rear leg knee kick

COMMON MISTAKES

MISTAKE 1: Raising the leg straight upward.
SOLUTION: Balance and the correct arcing motion are the most difficult to achieve with this kick. If you have trouble making the in-to-outward arc, start at waist level where it is easier to control your leg.

MISTAKE 2: Bending your torso or leaning backward.
SOLUTION: When your upper body is tilted and the muscles are tight, the arc of your kick becomes smaller and you lose your balance. Focus on keeping your head upright and your shoulders relaxed. Emphasize flexibility rather than power.

• REMEMBER

1. Keep your head upright.
2. Relax your shoulders.
3. After kicking, let your foot go and repose your body naturally.

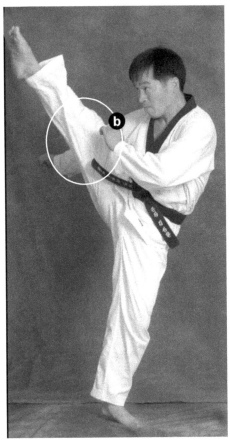

• AVOID

1. Bending the torso (**a**)
2. Raising the leg straight upward (**b**)
3. Leaning backward

INSIDE CRESCENT KICK

PURPOSE

Inside crescent kick is used to strike a close-range target located in front of you. The out-to-inward trajectory makes it a good surprise attack. The target is usually the face or side of the head. It is also useful for chopping downward on the clavicle area.

KEY POINTS

Slap the target with your foot from the outside. Relax your shoulders, erect your spine and raise your foot lightly before releasing it into the target. Use the element of surprise to catch your opponent off guard.

STRIKING AREA

Bottom of the foot, heel

TARGETS

1. face
2. chest
3. clavicle

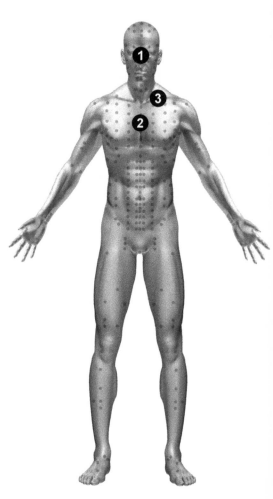

HOW TO

1. From fighting stance, shift your weight to the front leg.
2. Bring your rear leg up about 15° outside of the target line. Snap the inner bottom of the foot inward in an arc to the target (usually the face or head). You can impact the target horizontally or at a diagonally downward angle.
3. To finish, continue through the target and return to fighting stance.

Your head should be at the vertical center at all times while your hands travel in the opposite direction of the kick for balance and power.

*Kick only flexible targets with inside or outside crescent kick. Kicking an immovable target can damage your knee or hip.

APPLICATIONS

Inside crescent kick has a surprise element that can be used to intimidate an eager opponent. It is useful when the opponent attacks your middle or low section, when he lands short after an attack, or when he has a weapon in his hand. The swinging of your foot should be well timed to hit a moving target. Strive for a light, fast and precise kick.

SPORT APPLICATION:
Right: Counter your opponent's punch to the stomach with an inside crescent kick to the temple.

SPORT APPLICATION:
Left: Immediately after the opponent finishes a backfist strike, throw an inside crescent kick to the face.

SELF-DEFENSE APPLICATION:
Below: Use an inside crescent kick to kick the forearm and block the assailant's knife thrust.

COMMON MISTAKES

MISTAKE 1: The most serious mistake is incorrect distribution of weight. *SOLUTION:* If you throw your foot forward too heavily, you expose your face to the opponent. If you lean back while kicking to move away from the incoming opponent, you fall backward. To avoid these errors, make sure that you use short agile footwork before lifting your foot and stay centered over your kicking leg.

• REMEMBER

1. Center yourself for balance before kicking.
2. Move your feet first to create optimal distance from the opponent and then kick.

• AVOID

1. Tilting the torso (**ⓐ**)
2. Over-rotation of the body
3. Wide arc of the kick
4. Throwing your weight forward

PURPOSE

Axe kick is primarily used to strike the head and a successful kick often results in a knockout. It is also effective as a counterattack against a roundhouse kick or in stopping a reckless opponent from rushing in on you.

KEY POINTS

Have a firm base (standing leg) for stability and shift your weight completely onto your standing leg to fully relax the muscles in your kicking leg. Raise your leg as quickly as possible to gain maximum height.

STRIKING AREA

Bottom of the foot, heel

TARGETS

1. face
2. clavicle
3. sternum

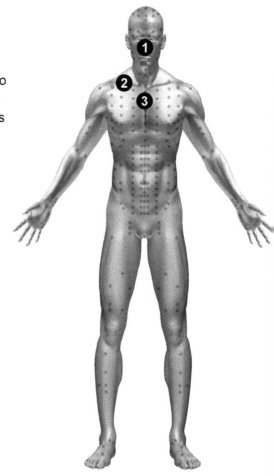

HOW TO

1. From fighting stance, shift your weight fully to your front leg.
2. Bring your leg straight up on the target line with the knee slightly bent. Bring your knee to your chest and, when your foot reaches maximum height, snap it downward.

* You may raise your leg with the knee straight and chop downward the foot, keeping the knee straight. Axe kick may be executed with a snapping force or a chopping force, depending on the application.

As the leg raises vertically, the arms spread horizontally for balance. The entire body should move in unison to generate maximum force in the foot at impact. Tuck your chin down to direct the force of your body forward and prevent leaning back during kicking.

The higher the foot goes, the more power your kick produces. The power of axe kick originates in a large range of motion.

APPLICATIONS

The ultimate goal of axe kick is to strike a stationary or moving target at a perpendicular angle, utilizing the advantage of the length of the leg. Although it requires greater distance to be effective, it is especially useful against a shorter weapon. Thus it is popular in martial art competition to stop punchers and to create distance between you and the opponent.

SPORT APPLICATIONS

Use axe kick to the head as a close quarters counterattack against punching.

Axe kick is a good way to make the opponent move away from you, to create distance or stop an aggressive opponent.

An axe kick is a safe and powerful technique against a crouching opponent.

SELF-DEFENSE APPLICATION

TRAINING TIPS

AXE KICK COMBINATIONS:

- Axe kick + roundhouse kick
- Axe kick + side kick
- Axe kick + punch + roundhouse kick
- Axe kick + hopping front kick

ACTIVE MUSCLE RELAXATION

When you first begin practicing kicks like axe kick and raising kick, you might find it quite hard to relax your leg muscles, which will cause your kicking height to suffer. Because the leg is so heavy, it can seem nearly impossible to lift it with the lightness necessary to kick above your head while maintaining your posture and balance. To help you relax your muscles while practicing, try using a support, like a stretching bar, to assist with your balance. The stretching bar will help you anchor your upper body position and take some of the stress off your standing leg, allowing you to relax your kicking leg fully.

1. Hold the bar with your rear side hand and anchor your posture with your rear hand and front leg.

2. Swing your rear leg up and down a few times, beginning small and increasing in height progressively.

3. As you feel your kicking leg relax and lighten, raise it once to maximum height, then return to step 2. Repeat 10 times on each side.

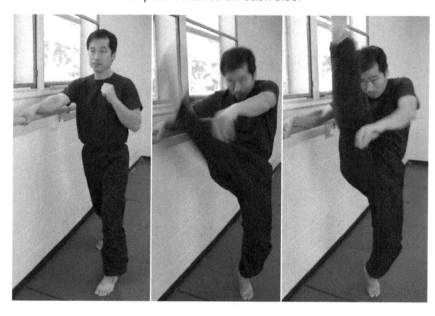

HEIGHT DRILLS

Using a visual, physical target is a good way to increase your kicking height and to keep track of your improvement. If you are having difficulty improving, take a measured progressive approach. For example, set a goal of increasing your target height one-quarter inch every other day. If you can achieve these small increases regularly, you'll have increased your kicking height by 12 inches in about 3 months!

COMMON MISTAKES

MISTAKE 1: The most serious mistake with axe kick is overworking your muscles. When you try too hard to raise your leg high, the muscles get tight leading to pain and frustration.

SOLUTION: The easiest solution is to lower your target height and build up progressively. If you have prolonged pain in your muscles, rest and heal first, then begin at a height you feel comfortable with and build up gradually as described on pages 126-127.

MISTAKE 2: Pulling the toes of the kicking foot.

SOLUTION: If you lift your leg with your foot, you'll find that you have to pull your toes back to create enough lifting force. Instead, lift your leg from your hip and thigh, keeping your foot and ankle relaxed.

• REMEMBER

1. Create good posture to leave the kicking leg free of tension.
2. Plant your standing foot firmly for stability.
3. Build the height of your kick progressively.
4. Raise your leg straight upward quickly and drop your foot on the target.

A quick, flexible axe kick is a powerful weapon in sparring. The secrets to developing a reliable axe kick are regular stretching and consistent practice to enhance height and precision.

• AVOID

1. Pulling the toes, which causes the hamstring muscle to tighten (**a**)
2. Lifting the heel, decreasing stability (**b**)
3. Over-stretching, causing a loss of balance and opening yourself to counterattacks (**c**)

PURPOSE

Whip kick is used to strike the opponent across the head or face. In general, use a back leg whip kick for attacking and a front leg whip kick for counterattacking. Setting up the proper distance and height is the key to success in using the whip kick as a counterattack. The best option: just as the opponent finishes his kicking attack, throw a whip kick counter to his face.

KEY POINTS

Whip kick is a good way to strike your opponent with a surprise counterattack. Wait until your opponent exposes his face after an attack and then strike.

STRIKING AREA

Bottom of the foot, toes

TARGETS

1. face
2. temple
3. neck

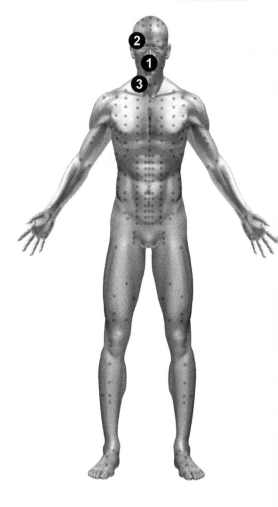

HOW TO

1. From fighting stance, shift your weight to the front leg.
2. Bring your knee up pointing toward the target.
3. Pivot your standing foot and align your body perpendicular to the target, with your shin parallel to the floor and knee tightly folded.
4. Raise your knee as you unfold it and hook your foot across the target, pulling your foot toward your buttocks as you open your hip. Kick through the target and return to fighting stance.

*Kick horizontally across
the target with maximum
range of motion.*

*The horizontal alignment
of the hip shown here
enables you to kick higher
and wider.*

APPLICATIONS

A front leg whip kick is faster and easier to do than a rear leg whip kick. The most effective targets for whip kick are the jaw, cheek, temple, and neck. The key to throwing a successful whip kick is timing; you must react as soon as you see an open target. If you delay even a fraction of a second, your opponent will be too close or too far away to strike. When you practice whip kick, focus on a quick initiation of the kick and a direct path of movement to the target.

As the opponent steps in, throw a front leg whip kick to the jaw.

When the opponent lands after an attack, throw a front leg whip kick to the ear.

SELF-DEFENSE APPLICATION: Use a whip kick to the neck of an opponent preparing to attack.

MARTIAL ARTS APPLICATION: *Right: In a pre-arranged step sparring technique, grab the opponent as you kick over his punching arm.*

SPORT APPLICATION: *Below: As the opponent raises his leg for axe kick, launch a whip kick counterattack.*

RANGE OF MOTION

Range of motion, or ROM, is the measurable distance between the flexed position and the extended position of a joint. The greater the ROM of your kick is, the more power it generates. ROM can be increased by improving flexibility of the muscles in the legs and torso, and of the joints in the hip, spine and knee.

Top: whip kick practice to a hand-held target is an excellent way to improve ROM in a safe way. Avoid kicking immovable targets with whip kick.

Right: for advanced practitioners, additional follow through after a whip kick is a good way to increase power.

The greater the range of motion in your kick, the more power your kick generates; the more flexible you are, the greater range of motion you have.
The exercise shown here will increase the range of motion and flexibility of your hips for whip kick.

Continue raising your leg, with your toes pointed. The final position of this stretch is the same as the moment of impact for whip kick. This stretches the hip joint and the muscles in the front of the leg.

Begin to rotate your upper body to the right and open your hips as you raise your leg. This strengthens the muscles of the buttocks while opening the hips.

Holding the bar, point your toes and lift your right leg to the left, across your body. This stretches your hip and torso muscles.

COMMON MISTAKES

MISTAKE 1: Exposing your torso to the opponent during or after kicking.
SOLUTION: This is generally caused by poor posture or kicking too slowly. Be sure to keep your hands and arms close to your body in a guarding position, whip your kick quickly across the target and avoid spinning your torso toward the target after kicking.

MISTAKE 2: Kicking too short or with limited range of motion.
SOLUTION: The main causes are lack of flexibility and coordination. Whip kick is a complex movement that works against the natural tendencies of the body because it forces the spine to bend backward. Improving the flexibility and strength of your back and ab muscles in addition to stretching your legs and hips will correct this problem.

• REMEMBER
1. Keep your head straight.
2. Firmly plant the standing foot.
3. Pivot your foot for a quick and smooth rotation of the body.
4. Keep your kicking leg free of tension.

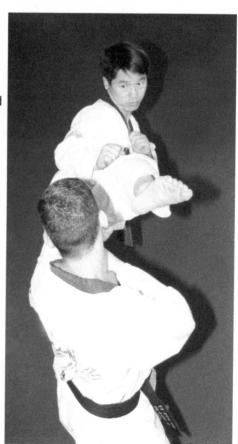

Extend your foot about 6-12 inches in front of the intended target. More than this and your kick will be too wide. Less and you will not have enough space to generate a powerful slapping motion prior to contacting the target.

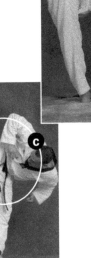

• AVOID

1. Kicking too high (**a**)
2. Exposing your torso to the opponent after kicking (**b**)
3. Kicking too slowly and exposing vital targets to the opponent (**c**)

PURPOSE

Twist kick is an irregular type of kick which travels in the opposite direction of conventional kicks. The power and effectiveness of twist kick come from coiling and uncoiling the body from an unusual angle, however this also makes it vulnerable. The danger is that you may expose vital targets on your torso after kicking, so you need to protect your body during and after kicking.

KEY POINTS

Keep your head and standing foot mostly fixed while rotating your chest and hips sequentially in an outward U shape.

STRIKING AREA

Ball, blade, instep

TARGETS

1. face
2. temple
3. neck
4. rib cage
5. stomach
6. inner thigh
7. inner knee

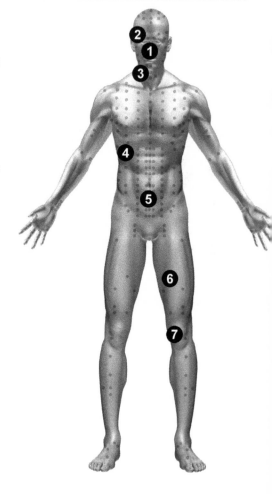

HOW TO

1. From fighting stance, shift your weight to the front leg.
2. Bring your knee up and twist your body slightly inward, beginning with your chest followed immediately by your hips. As you do so, raise your kicking leg with the foot and knee tilting about 30 to 45 degrees upward.
3. Pivot your standing foot, reverse the rotation of your hip and torso outward, unfold your knee outward, and kick outward-upward with the outside, ball or blade of your foot. All of these steps happen sequentially and almost simultaneously, like coiling and releasing a spring.

VARIATIONS

Twist kick is useful for kicking soft or vulnerable targets such as the inner thigh, groin, lower abdomen, solar plexus, neck, chin, nose, ears, and mandibular joint. For kicking to the lower abdomen, solar plexus or neck, striking with the ball of the foot (photo 1) is most effective due to its penetrating power. For most of the other targets, the outer side of the foot (photo 2) is effective due to its wide striking surface area.

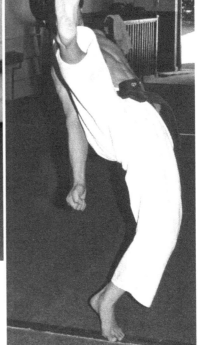

When striking with the ball of the foot, rotate your body fully so that the ball contacts the target area as sharply as possible.

When striking with the outer side of the foot, put your body weight behind the kick for additional power.

APPLICATIONS

This is a kick that is rarely used, so the element of surprise is one of its primary advantages. Use it to shock or confuse your opponent then follow up with a powerful combination such as an elbow strike or round-house kick.

Left: A long twist kick to the groin can stop an advancing assailant.

Below: A good time for a twist kick is after the opponent misses with a forward attack.

SELF-DEFENSE APPLICATIONS

HIP JOINT EXERCISES

Because of its unusual path of striking, twist kick can result in injuries to the muscles and joints of the hip or groin. You can improve your flexibility by doing these simple exercises:

Vertical foot lifting:
Alternately lift your right and left foot to hip level. Inhale while resting and exhale when you lift your foot. You can do this in-place or while moving around the room, interspersing the knee lifts with footwork. Repeat 3 sets of 20 repetitions, alternating sides.

* After the exercises, shake your legs to release tension in your hips. You can stand and shake one leg at a time or sit on the floor and shake both legs simultaneously.

Outward knee lifting:
Lift your knee outward, alternating legs. Raise your foot only to knee level. As you raise your knee and open your hip, your body will twist naturally, creating a coiling motion.

COMMON MISTAKES

The most common mistake is putting too much power in the kick, resulting in a breakdown in posture and inefficient use of your energy as well as potential joint injuries. To correct this, hold a stretching bar and practice slowly without force until you master the path of the kicking motion and can generate force from range of motion rather than muscle power.

• REMEMBER

1. Center your body.
2. Generate power from your hips.
3. Keep your base foot firmly planted.
4. Keep your head as straight as possible.

• AVOID

1. Kicking too far past target
2. Breaking the vertical center (both illustrated by photo **a**)

TWISTING POWER

Twisting power comes from coiling and uncoiling the muscles of the torso. Before practicing twisting outward with your kick, you can develop your twisting skills by kicking upward first.

1. Bring your knee forward at a tilted angle. Your arms swing to the left initially and return to this position naturally.

2. Raise your knee to your chest, while pivoting your standing foot.

3. Kick at a target directly on your centerline. Note the difference between this target and the one on page 146, which lies about one foot outside the body.

PURPOSE

Pushing kick is used to stop an incoming opponent or to push away an opponent to create space for a stronger attack. Chamber your knee quickly and push the opponent's lower abdomen or thigh. You can also raise your nearly straight leg and push straight forward. The goal of this kick is to destroy the opponent's equilibrium.

KEY POINTS

Attack the opponent's center of gravity. Don't kick too high; kick the middle of the body. Maintain your balance by bringing your arms and torso forward with your kicking momentum.

STRIKING AREA

Ball, bottom of the foot

TARGETS

1. lower abdomen
2. femoral crease
3. thigh
4. solar plexus

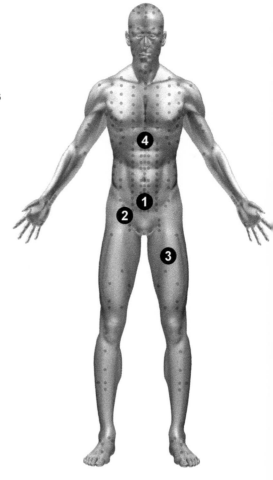

HOW TO

1. From fighting stance, shift your weight to the front leg.
2. Bring your knee forward toward the target.
3. Raise your knee to chest level and push your foot forward. Keep your upper body erect and bring your body weight forward with the momentum of the kick.

* You may push with the ball or bottom of the foot.

VARIATIONS

Pushing kick is a timing-sensitive technique. Use it to take advantage of an opponent who rushes in recklessly or to push away an indecisive opponent as he hesitates. If you need to react quickly to an opportunity, use a front foot pushing kick; for a powerful push, use the rear foot. The former creates speedy action; the latter an aggressive attack.

1 + **2** = *hopping front foot pushing kick as a quick counter*

1 + **3** = *rear foot pushing kick for a powerful attack*

APPLICATIONS

Pushing kick is a tactical skill used to better control distance in a fight by unbalancing the opponent's center of gravity. Push a joint, such as the knee or hip crease. According to the situation, you can push straight forward with a front kick, horizontally with a side kick, or diagonally with a hybrid of the two. The fundamental principles of execution for all of these applications are the same.

SELF-DEFENSE APPLICATION:
Use a diagonal pushing kick to the knee to intimidate an opponent.

SPORT APPLICATION:
Use a long pushing kick to the opponent's torso to create space for a follow up attack.

SELF-DEFENSE APPLICATION:
Use a *side pushing kick to the rib cage while avoiding the assailant's lunging attack.*

SELF-DEFENSE APPLICATION: Left: A stomping push kick to the groin can incapacitate a downed assailant allowing you to escape to safety.

SPORT APPLICATION: Below: a long pushing kick with the ball of the foot negates the opponent's punches.

COMMON MISTAKES

MISTAKE 1: Losing balance during the kick.

SOLUTION: Keep your standing knee slightly bent and don't overextend your kicking leg. Also, bring your upper body forward with the kick and keep your arms close to your body; don't lean backward.

MISTAKE 2: Telegraphing your movement.

SOLUTION: Begin your kick like front kick and push at the last moment. Don't make your initial movement too large.

• REMEMBER

1. Push through the target.
2. Bend supporting knee.
3. Use your bodyweight.
4. Control your torso.

• AVOID

1. Opening your arms
2. Leaning backward (**a**)
3. Overextending your kick (**b**)
4. Kicking above the waist (**c**)

WEIGHT SHIFTING FOR PUSHING KICK

Pushing kick requires coordination and flexibility to deliver power. Here are examples of exercises for rear (1-3) and front (4-6) foot pushing kicks using a heavy bag.

1. From fighting stance shift your weight to the front leg.
2. Bring your rear knee to the front at chest level and lean your body forward as you come into contact with the bag.
3. Push your foot as far into the target as you can without breaking your posture. Be sure to bring your upper body forward with the kick and keep your guard up.
4. From fighting stance, hop your rear foot to your front foot.
5. Upon arrival of the rear foot, quickly raise your front foot, keeping your body turned slightly sideways.
6. Stretch your kicking leg into the target and lean your body forward as you push the bag.

FLYING SIDE KICK

PURPOSE

Flying side kick is used to strike a runaway or charging opponent. The dynamic appearance of flying side kick makes it popular for demonstrations as well. The ultimate goal of practicing this kick is to attain maximum jumping distance and height. It requires muscular strength and coordination to achieve complete synchronization of the body while in the air.

KEY POINTS

The main force of flying side kick comes from momentum and the extension of the leg on impact. When you jump, make your body compact and thrust your leg at the target just prior to impact.

STRIKING AREA

Blade, ball, bottom of the foot, heel

TARGETS

1. head
2. neck
3. chest
4. solar plexus

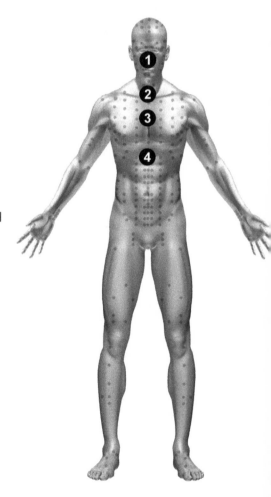

HOW TO

1. From fighting stance, size up the distance and height of the target.

2. Step forward and take as many steps as you need to pace yourself.

3. At the point of jumping, pivot your body 180° and elevate your torso as high as you can, while raising your kicking knee to chest level.

4. Just before reaching the peak of the jump, bring both knees close to your body and let your compact body "fly" toward the target.

5. At the peak, snap your primary foot out in a side kick. Keep your other leg tucked in close to your buttocks to augment the flying momentum.

Upward flying side kick is more advanced than conventional side kick and requires outstanding flexibility and strength of the leg muscles. The torso leans back more than horizontal flying side kick to allow the kicking leg to strike upward.

APPLICATIONS

Flying side kick is powerful because it delivers the weight of the entire body, which is propelled by the momentum of running and jumping. When used with control and coordination, it can knock an opponent to the ground. Flying side kick requires a long approach, so it is more commonly used for demonstrations and board breaking than in practical applications.

MARTIAL ARTS
APPLICATIONS

Flying side kick to the heavy bag is the safest way to practice full power kicks, to learn to align your body in the air, and to obtain instant feedback on impact.

Top: A short flying side kick against a lunging opponent can take his breath away and establish dominance.

Below: A quick flying side kick to the arm can momentarily paralyze the muscles.

Flying side kick is an excellent technique for demonstrations and board breaking. Practice in front of mirror to create a proper form and with a light target (such as a handheld target) to develop accuracy.

* When executing a flying side kick without a firm target to strike, for example in a demonstration, jump, extend your leg and hold it in the air rather than kicking to full extension. Putting too much power in a flying side kick without a proper target to absorb the impact can result in joint injuries.

PERFECTING YOUR FORM

• Build strong muscles in the legs through squats, lunges and jumping drills.
• Strengthen the stomach muscles with sit-ups and crunches.
• Jump rope or run in sand to strengthen your knees and ankles.
• Practice running rhythmically and jumping after a consistent number of steps.
• Align your body in a triangular shape (head, kicking foot and supporting knee as shown below) at the peak of your jump.

COMMON MISTAKES

The most common mistake occurs in jumping—either in lowering the torso to the side or rushing the sequence of movements. To correct this, follow a natural sequence: run to pick up momentum, lift your rear knee forward as high as you can, pivot your torso using the momentum of the rising knee, stretch the kicking leg toward the target while bringing up the supporting leg up. Begin from a low jump and build up in height. Be sure to build your leg strength sufficiently before attempting this kick.

• REMEMBER

1. Elevate your torso first.
2. Raise your kicking knee high.
3. Pivot your body to the side and align your torso and legs on one plane.
4. Make your body compact while in the air and unfold it when kicking.

• AVOID

1. Jumping too far or too high
2. Dropping your non-kicking leg (**a**)
3. Rushing your jump or kick
4. Kicking with too much power (**b**)
5. Lowering your torso to the side or rear (**c**)
6. Opening your arms too wide (**c**)

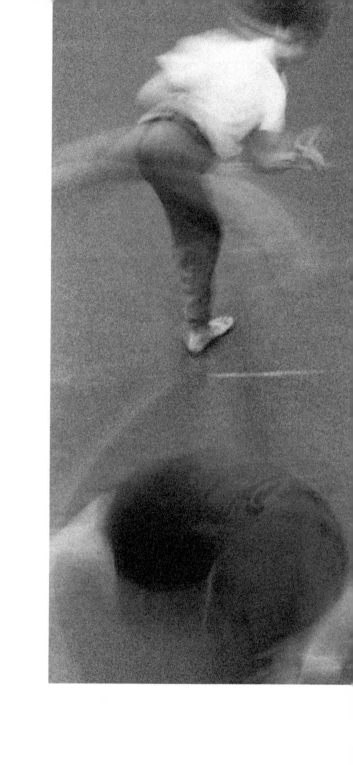

SPINNING & TURNING KICKS

The spinning and turning kicks in this section are based on what you have learned so far. Spinning or turning kicks involve quick rotation of the body while maintaining proper form.

Three important elements for successful spinning kicks are focus, balance and agility. Focus is enhanced by spotting the target before and after turning your body and following a direct kicking path to the target. For balance, keep your center of the gravity lower than normal and stay relaxed. For agility, concentrate on moving intuitively rather than analytically. To succeed, be in tune with your natural awareness rather than worrying about your mistakes.

PURPOSE

In competition back kick is very often used for counterattacking against roundhouse kick or as a surprise attack. Back kick's power comes from the rotation of the body, however deceptive execution adds to the kick's effectiveness. Since turning the body is risky, you should spot the target immediately after turning and be on guard at all times.

KEY POINTS

Start from a sideways stance to reduce the initial movement of your body and initiation time. Rotate your hip first and then throw your foot directly to the target, delivering your entire bodyweight, which is magnified by the spinning motion.

STRIKING AREA

Blade, bottom of the foot, ball, heel

TARGETS

1. abdomen
2. solar plexus
3. neck
4. face
5. kidney

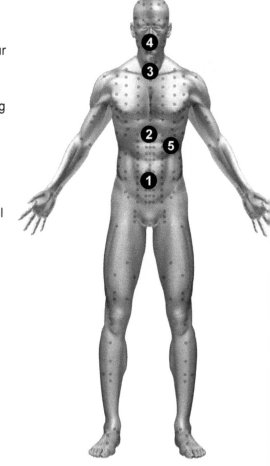

HOW TO

1. From fighting stance, shift your weight to the neutral position.

2. Turn your head and spot the target over your shoulder as you rotate your body so your back is to the target. Chamber your knee with your kicking foot next to the standing knee.

3. Shoot your foot out while watching the target over your shoulder and protecting your vital targets with your arms. After kicking, return to the original position or step down into fighting stance.

Keep your head upright for optimal balance.

Spot the target over your shoulder while maintaining your equilibrium.

Utilize your arms to center your body and to protect your torso while turning.

Keep your foot under your hip along the centerline to protect your groin against a counterattack.

VARIATIONS

Variations of the back kick are most useful when applied in the least expected manner. Back kick from the ground, for instance, is an effective technique to surprise or confuse an opponent who expects you to stand and fight. As soon as you are done kicking, use your opponent's momentary distraction to get up and protect yourself from standing position.

Right: From the kneeling position, put your hands on the floor so that you have a firm triangular base of one knee and two hands to support a back kick to the lower stomach of an advancing opponent. Do not turn your body; keep it sideways so that your groin and face are covered.

Below: Keep your kicking foot tilted so your toes are lower than your heel.

Keep your head up and your eyes on the target. Bend your kicking knee slightly to facilitate balance and the ability to move quickly after kicking.

BODY ALIGNMENT

To hit a moving opponent, you need to spin and kick quickly. For accuracy in such a fast and complex movement, your sight line, foot, and target should be aligned on one plane. To perfect your kick, slow supported-kicking drills (right) can help you develop muscle memory. The more familiar your body is with the sequence of the kick's movements, the more precise your kick will be.

Three point stabilization (1 foot and 2 hands) enhances posture and accuracy while developing muscle memory.

APPLICATIONS

Back kick is a versatile kick that is primarily used to stop an incoming opponent or counterattack against a circular kick (roundhouse kick) or a vertical kick (axe kick). You can use it at short or medium distance, but avoid using it from long range. Retract your foot immediately and stay away from or move in close to your opponent after kicking.

SELF-DEFENSE APPLICATION:
Left: When an assailant grabs you from the rear, take one step forward and kick while leaning forward to gain space.

SPORT APPLICATION:
Below: As the opponent lands after jumping roundhouse kick, counter with a short back kick.

Left: As soon as the opponent completes his left turn kick and drops his body forward, counter with a right back kick.

Below: Against a left axe kick, when the opponent drops his head forward, counter with a back kick.

SPORT APPLICATIONS

MARTIAL ARTS APPLICATIONS

A powerful back kick is an audience pleasing demonstration skill. If you time your kick and the reaction of your partner well, the result is awesome, artistic and entertaining.

Back kick on the ground is frequently used in arranged step sparring in traditional schools and is a good way for students to practice the correct angle, distance and force control for back kick.

COMMON MISTAKES

MISTAKE 1: The most common mistake is exposure of the hip, on which your opponent can land a pushing kick counter.

SOLUTION: This problem can be solved by turning your body more to the side and aligning the kicking foot, hip and shoulder on one plane.

MISTAKE 2: Another common problem is exposure of the groin and chest areas to the opponent's counterattack.

SOLUTION: This can be solved by closing your chest a little bit (turning it away from the target) and keeping the toes of the kicking foot slightly lower than the heel.

• REMEMBER

1. Turn your body to the side.
2. Shift your weight to neutral position.
3. Spot the target over your shoulder.
4. Align your body for maximum length.
5. Withdraw your foot in reverse of the way you kicked.

To kick higher it is acceptable to lower your torso, however, you should still look at the target, align your body on one plane and keep your weight neutrally centered over your standing leg.

• AVOID

1. Exposure of your hip
2. Exposure of your face and chest
3. Misalignment of the body
4. Over-rotation

PURPOSE

Turn kick is used to attack deceptively, to add the power of spinning to roundhouse kick, or to counterattack while retreating. It is powerful enough to knock down an opponent and effective for penetrating defense. It is usually used in combination with double or triple kicks, a roundhouse kick or a back kick.

KEY POINTS

Once you spot an opening, don't hesitate; turn and kick in one smooth committed motion. Stalling during the turn hinders balance and naturalness. Keep your torso upright and lower your center of the gravity.

STRIKING AREA

Instep, ball, shin

TARGETS

1. stomach
2. solar plexus
3. kidney
4. liver
5. neck
6. face
7. temple

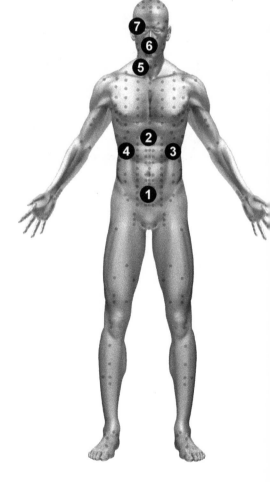

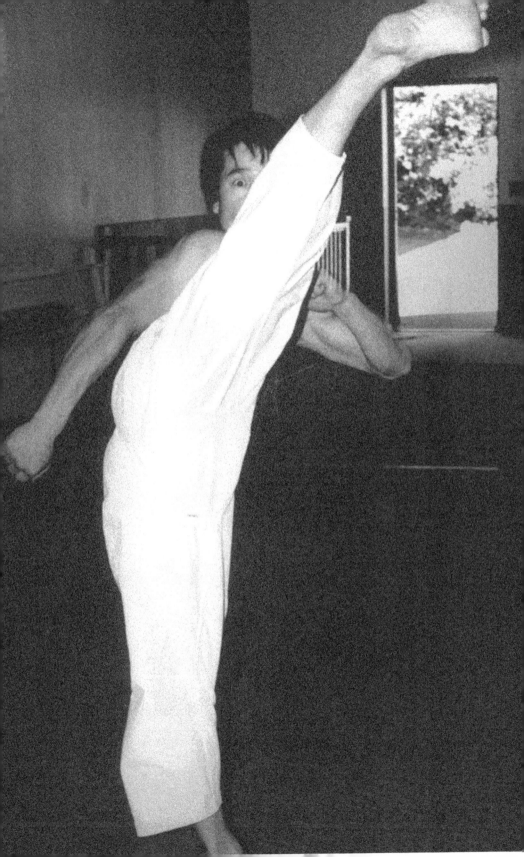

HOW TO

1. From fighting stance, shift your weight to the front leg.

2. Pivot your front foot, rotate your hip to the rear, toward the target, and then turn your torso in the same direction. Spot the target over your shoulder. Move your rear foot forward.

3. As your rear foot crosses your body, rotate your hip quickly toward the target, and chamber your kicking leg in the air.

4. Release your foot to the target and rotate your hip fully into your kick for maximum delivery of power.

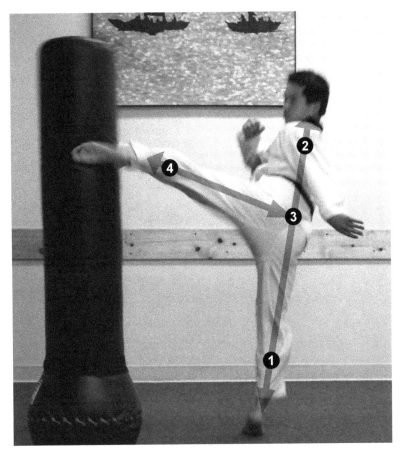

Ideally, at the moment of impact, your torso and legs should make a triangular shape with the primary force traveling to the kicking leg. In the illustration above your standing foot and leg are the power base (1), your front side shoulder is the power stabilizer (2), your hip is the power hub (3), and your kicking leg and foot are the power transmitters (4).

BALANCE POINT

N MOTION, LITTLE 'HINGS MATTER:

Avoid crossing your feet.
Keep your knees slightly bent.
Avoid long strides. Use short, quick footwork when turning.

APPLICATIONS

Turn kick is mostly used in competition, either moving forward or while retreating. It is powerful and deceptive when done correctly, however, it is reserved for advanced practitioners due to the speed and coordination required. If you lose your balance while turning or misjudge the distance to the target, you'll find yourself in trouble. To avoid problems, maintain good posture, turn your body quickly and smoothly, and complete the kick in less than a second, preferably in a half second or less.

Moving faster than your opponent is the key to scoring with turn kick. To do so, you should try to perceive your opponent's intent to attack. Look for cues such as blinking, a sharp inhalation, lowering of the shoulder, movement the front foot, twitching the hip, etc. The above photo demonstrates a well timed turn kick, striking when the opponent's rear leg axe kick is at maximum height and his torso is vulnerable to a counterattack.

Left: Before the opponent completes his high round-house kick, counter with a quick turn kick.

Below: When an opponent hesitates, attack with a turn kick.

SPORT APPLICATIONS

Counter with a retreating turn kick as soon as your opponent lands after kicking.

COMMON MISTAKES

MISTAKE 1: Leaning the torso or head to the side.

SOLUTION: Avoid jerking your head when turning. Rotate your head and torso around the vertical axis that connects the top of your head and the center of the spine. Keep your head height level.

MISTAKE 2: Turning too widely or stepping in a zigzag pattern.

SOLUTION: If your turn is not made on a single line directly toward the target, you will find yourself out of position to hit the target. Rotate your hip first, spot the target over your shoulder and then turn so you have the target in sight at all times. Move on a straight line with your torso erect.

• REMEMBER

1. Rotate your hip first and let the other parts of the body follow.
2. Keep your head straight and rotate it smoothly to spot the target.
3. Relax your shoulders and allow your center of the gravity to guide you.

Above: at the moment of impact, the torso leans into the direction of the kick for additional power.

Left: the turn kick can be very powerful when the whole body works in sync.

Above: unbalanced turn kick

Left: miscalculation of the distance

• AVOID
1. Leaning the torso or head off the target line (**a**)
2. Jerky turning of the torso or head
3. Large turning motion (**a**)
4. Zig zag stepping, stepping off the force line, poor distance control (**b**)
5. Banging knees with the opponent

PURPOSE

Spin whip kick is used to counterattack against roundhouse kick or axe kick. It can also be a powerful deceptive knockout attack. The knockout power of spin whip kick comes from the turning momentum of the body. It is stunning and devastating in effectiveness because it has the greatest range of motion of any kick.

KEY POINTS

Timing and distance are the primary factors for a successful spin whip kick. Power is secondary because without proper timing and distance, a powerful spin whip kick is risky and useless.

STRIKING AREA

Ball, heel, bottom of the foot

TARGETS

1. temple
2. jaw
3. face
4. neck

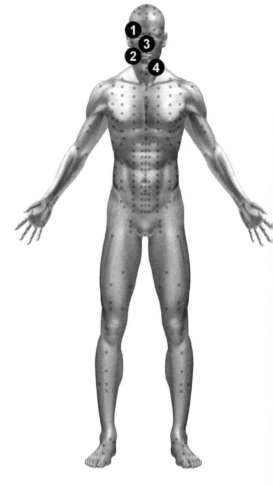

HOW TO

1. From fighting stance, shift your weight to the neutral position.

2. Rotate your body to the rear, chamber the rear leg and look over your shoulder.

3. Raise your kicking leg and keep your body as compact as possible before kicking.

4. Shoot your foot toward the target, about 6-12 inches in front of it, then hook across and through the target. Continue the spin and the trajectory of the kicking leg, returning to fighting stance.

Left: Spin whip kick follows a fan shaped path, lashing the target as if with a whip. The power of this kick comes from a combination of the large range of motion of the foot and the central axis of the torso, around which the foot moves. The torso functions as a stabilizer and your standing foot acts as the pivot.

Below: Diagonal sit-ups build the muscles of the torso used in spin whip kick. As your muscles become stronger, try a larger range of motion during the sit-up, which will increase the range of motion of your kick.

APPLICATIONS

The primary target for spin whip kick is the head, which means you should be flexible and fast. Generally, you can kick higher when you kick fast; you can kick fast when you have muscular stability. Through strength and flexibility training, you can attain both. That said, all you need to do is stay alert yet relaxed and look for or make an opportunity of perfect timing. Avoid hitting the torso with spin whip kick to prevent knee and back injuries.

SPORT APPLICATION: Spin whip kick is popular in Taekwondo competition. It is effective as a counterattack when your opponent attacks with an axe kick or roundhouse kick. The best time to counter is when his technique is at its peak. If you fail to do so, strike as his foot lands and his head leans forward.

SPORT APPLICATION: Use *spin whip kick to strike the temple as your opponent steps in to attack.*

SELF-DEFENSE APPLICATION: *After the assailant completes a wide lunging attack, counter with a spin whip kick to the head, meeting force with force.*

Above: A spin whip kick across the back of the knees can be used from the ground to take down an opponent.

Below: If you've been knocked down, counter your opponent's charge with a spin whip kick from the ground.

As the opponent approaches to grab you, stop him with a spin whip kick to the head.

BALANCE POINT

60 ° BALANCE:

pin whip kick is one of several
vanced kicks that requires a 360° turn
the body. If you have practiced the
her turning and spinning kicks in this
apter, you should have developed the
undation skills for a full turn.

perfect your turning, focus on the
llowing:
Stand in a neutral fighting stance
eight equally on both legs).
Rotate your hip, torso and head in
equence.
With the turning momentum let the
ar foot "slide" around your body.
Repeat #1-3, getting progressively
ster. Aim for less than 1/2 second.

SELF-DEFENSE APPLICATIONS

TARGET KICKING DRILLS:

Practicing spinning whip kick on a heavy bag or a fixed target can result in a serious knee or back injury. Instead, use a flexible target like a handheld target or speed bag to enhance your accuracy and timing.

Left: Use a hand held kicking target to practice accuracy at different target heights. You can kick at a horizontal, upward or downward angle.

Below: The speed bag resembles a human head, providing realistic feedback when kicked.

ISOTONIC/ISOMETRIC WHIP KICK DRILL:

Using a combination of isotonic and isometric exercises, you can increase the flexibility, strength and range of motion in your legs and hip.

This combination of isotonic (muscular contraction where the muscle maintains relatively constant tension while the length changes) and isometric (muscular contraction against resistance while the length of the muscle remains the same) training methods is recommended for intermediate and advanced practitioners.

1. Hold the bar with both hands. Shift your weight to the left leg. Raise the right leg to the rear slowly and hold at a 45° angle. Point the toes and stretch the muscles in the front of the leg while tensing the muscles in the right buttock and rear of the leg. Hold for 1 minute.

2. Bring the right leg forward with the toes pointed and the muscles in the front of the thigh tensed while the muscles in the rear of the leg rest. Hold for 1 minute.

3. Raise your right leg to the rear while lowering your torso. Keep the toes pointed and feel the tension in the right buttock and right side of the torso. Rest the muscles in the front of the thigh. Hold for 1 minute.

4. With your right knee bent, move your leg horizontally back and forth. Increase the range of motion of the hip joint as you progress. Repeat 20 times.

Practice this exercises on both sides, 3 times a week.

COMMON MISTAKES

The most common mistakes are in centering and balancing. When your kick has too much power, it becomes out of control. Your body loses balance and thus misses the target. The centering diagram below shows the sequence of motions for spin whip kick:

1. hip rotation
2. torso rotation
3. head turn
4. leg folding
5. kicking impact
6. follow throw

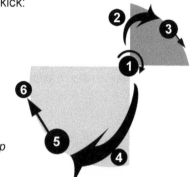

You may rotate your torso first, then the hip and leg. Choose what works best for you.

• REMEMBER

1. Center your body.
2. Spot the target before kicking.
3. Relax while moving.
4. Focus your power at impact.

• AVOID

1. Kicking too powerfully without accuracy
2. Tilting the head (**a**)
3. Over-rotation of the body (**b**)
4. Kicking in a wide arc

HOPPING KICKS

Hopping is a graduated tactic between stepping-in and jumping. Hopping should be short, light, and quick and may be done with a straight, circular or spinning kick. Adding a hop to a kick generates powerful penetrating impact. Be sure to synchronize your entire body as one unit and hop-kick in one count. Ultimately, you should be able to hop and kick in less than one second.

PURPOSE

Hop kicks are used to stun the opponent, to decisively break into his defense, or to counterattack against a fast attacker. Your movement should be short and quick, hitting the target accurately. Hop kicks should be springy in action and stinging in impact. On the following pages are three examples of hop kicks. Experiment in your practice to develop others.

KEY POINTS

Kick with clear-cut precision and lightning speed. Coil your body as you move into the hop and uncoil it into the target as you kick. Always keep your supporting knee bent and charge your hop with aggressive energy.

STRIKING AREA

Ball, blade, instep, toes, bottom of the foot

TARGETS

1. groin
2. lower abdomen
3. solar plexus
4. chest
5. mouth
6. temple
7. rib cage
8. thigh
9. knee

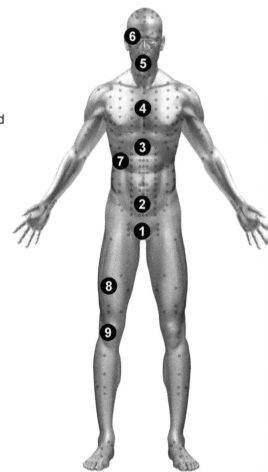

HOP ROUNDHOUSE KICK

HOW TO

1. From fighting stance, shift your weight to the front (right) leg.
2. Bring the rear foot forward, crossing in front of the front leg, and simultaneously twist the torso to the right and "coil" the body as you hop forward.
3. Rotate your hip into the target, uncoil your body and release your foot into the target. Strike the target before your bottom leg touches the ground. Land in fighting stance after kicking.

HOP SIDE KICK

HOW TO

1. From fighting stance, shift your weight to the front leg, and bound forward bringing your back leg to your front leg as you leave the ground.
2. As your body elevates, snap your foot toward the target, striking with the bottom or blade of the foot before the other foot touches the ground. Keep your body perpendicular to the target throughout your movement. Land in fighting stance.

HOP WHIP KICK

HOW TO

1. From fighting stance, shift your weight to the front leg while bringing the rear foot next to the front foot, bounding forward and elevating your body.

2. Raise your front leg and throw your whip kick, striking with the bottom of your foot before your other foot touches the ground. Land in fighting stance.

JUMPING KICKS

Jumping requires strong leg and abdomen muscles and complete commitment to the technique. To succeed, you need to jump suddenly and kick powerfully.

While hopping kicks are speedy techniques, jumping kicks are powerful attacks or counterattacks. However, jump kicks are impractical unless you have mastered the technique and have experience with a variety of situations and opponents. You should be able to sense, not just see and think, the perfect moment for a jumping kick. Be bold and focus on the timing of your kick. Generally, the best chance at success with a jumping kick is when your opponent is rigid, planning his next move, or tired. Avoid using jumping kicks against opponents who have superior footwork or agility, because they will take advantage of their superior skills to avoid your kick and counterattack.

PURPOSE

Jumping kicks are used to overpower, to counterattack, or to demonstrate advanced skills, such as a board breaking. The key to success is total body coordination and control of your bodyweight while in the air. Since they are fully committed techniques you should be absolutely certain in their execution. A half-hearted jumping kick results in disaster. You can improve your chances of success by reducing your opponent's mobility and stamina prior to a jump kick.

KEY POINTS

Once you commit to a jumping kick, never give up in the middle. If you've developed a jump kick to the point where you feel confident enough to use it against an opponent, be bold and fearless.

STRIKING AREA

Knee, ball, shin, toes, bottom of the foot

TARGETS

1. face
2. temple
3. neck
4. chest
5. solar plexus
6. kidney

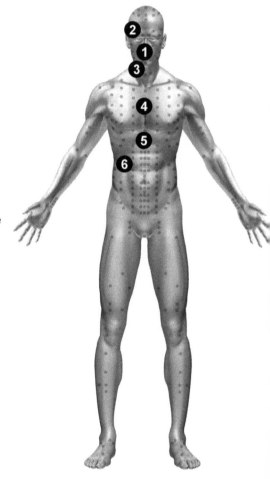

JUMPING FRONT KICK

HOW TO

1. From fighting stance, flex your knees slightly then start your jump by bringing your rear foot forward as you rotate your body 180° into the kick.

2. Bring both legs up with your knees bent, your arms close to your body and your kicking leg in front. Your feet should come up under your buttocks and your torso should be perpendicular to the ground to maintain your balance in the air.

3. At the peak of your jump, snap your front foot at the target while pulling your other leg up toward your buttocks. Hunch your head and torso slightly forward into the kick. Land in fighting stance.

JUMPING DROP KICK

HOW TO

1. From fighting stance, flex your knees slightly then start your jump by bringing your rear foot forward as you rotate your body 180° into the kick.

2. Bring both legs up with your knees bent, your arms close to your body and your kicking leg in front. Your feet should come up under your buttocks and your torso should be perpendicular to the ground to maintain your balance in the air.

3. At the peak of your jump, snap your front foot downward into the target while keeping your torso upright. Land in fighting stance.

VARIATION: Drop the ball of the foot downward into the abdomen or solar plexus on impact. Land in fighting stance.

JUMPING AXE KICK

HOW TO

1. From fighting stance, flex your knees slightly then start your jump by bringing your rear foot forward as you rotate your body 180° into the kick.
2. Bring both legs up with your knees bent, your arms close to your body and your kicking leg in front. Your feet should come up under your buttocks and your torso should be perpendicular to the ground to maintain your balance in the air.
3. At the peak of your jump, raise your front knee and foot as high as possible then drop it on the target, striking with the heel or bottom of the foot. Land in fighting stance.

JUMPING ROUNDHOUSE KICK

HOW TO

1. From fighting stance, lower your posture to prepare to jump.
2. Jump, twist your hips, and kick with the instep or toes in one smooth motion. As with other jumping kicks, keep your upper body and head upright and move your arms in sync with your body rotation.
3. For power, rotate your hip beyond the target. Land in fighting stance.

JUMPING SPLIT KICK

HOW TO

1. From a natural stance, jump straight upward, bringing your knees close to your chest. At the peak of your jump, split your legs to the sides and pull your toes back, kicking in an upward direction. Extend your hands at shoulder height as targets.

2. **VARIATION:** You may also drop both hands between your legs to gain additional height in your kick.

Keep your head up and look forward, rather than at the ground, throughout the jumping split kick. This will help you keep your torso upright and jump higher.

7

JUMP SPINNING & TURNING KICKS

Jump spinning and jump turning kicks are combinations of three elements: jump, spin or turn, and then kick. As complicated as it sounds, the principles are the same. Practice each segment separately at first and then practice how to transition between them seamlessly. When you use a jump spinning kick, don't procrastinate. Think and visualize before kicking. While you're kicking, only kick. When attacking with a jump spinning kick, you must surprise the opponent. When counterattacking, your goal is to make the opponent feel helpless by penetrating his defense either before, during and after his attack. Let him commit to his attack, and then strike. Be quick and agile.

PURPOSE

The main goal of jump spinning and turning kicks is to strike and penetrate deeply into the target. They are used for counterattacking, however, they may be used for attacking with a high success rate due to the novelty of their application. The target for circular kicks like jump turn kick and jump spinning whip kick is the head. For linear kicks like jump back kick, the target is the torso. Due to their riskiness, jump spinning kicks and jump turning kicks are reserved for advanced practitioners.

KEY POINTS

Accurately anticipate the height and distance of the final target. Fully commit to your technique and then follow through.

STRIKING AREA

Ball, heel, blade, toes, bottom of the foot

TARGETS

1. solar plexus
2. rib cage
3. chest
4. neck
5. face
6. jaw
7. temple

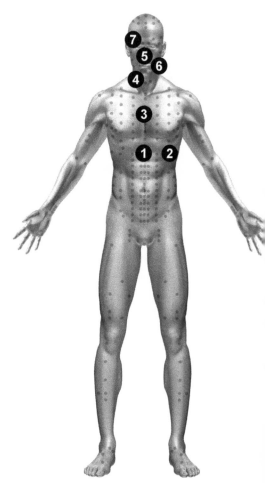

JUMP BACK KICK

HOW TO

1. From fighting stance, shift your weight to neutral position.

2. Jump, rotate your hips 180° to the rear, spot the target over your shoulder and chamber your legs by bending your knees and pulling your feet up toward your hips. Keep your torso upright.

3. Release your rear foot toward the target while keeping your torso upright and your other knee bent. Land in fighting stance.

PRACTICE TIP: Keep your kicking side shoulder, knee and foot aligned on one plane so your body travels directly to the target and doesn't swing around on a circular path.

JUMP TURN KICK

HOW TO

1. From fighting stance, shift your weight to the front leg and bend your knees slightly.
2. Rotate your body 180° to the rear and lift your rear foot, crossing your front leg as you begin to jump.
3. Continuing to turn and elevate, keep your torso upright and your knees bent.
4. Release your foot to the target while maintaining balance by finishing your rotation directly over your other leg. Land in fighting stance.

PRACTICE TIP: Practice on the ground slowly without jumping at first to get the mental image of this kick. Then turn and kick fast with a minimal jump. As you acquire precision and confidence, jump progressively higher.

JUMP SPIN WHIP KICK

HOW TO

1. From fighting stance, shift your weight to the neutral position.
2. In place, jump vertically, rotate your body to the rear, and either swing your rear leg in a circle to the rear or bend your knee and prepare to snap it at the target as you complete your rotation.
3. At the peak of your jump, snap or throw your foot at the target while keeping your torso upright and your supporting leg bent under you. Land in fighting stance.

PRACTICE TIP: Jumping requires leg strength. Spinning requires coordination to create torque in your hips. Kicking is a release of force created by both jumping and spinning. Visualize these three elements before kicking and when you kick, perform all three simultaneously.

✱ BALANCE POINT

EXPERIMENTAL TRAINING:

Experiment with ways to enhance awareness of your body and how it works. Here are some suggested training experiments:

1. Verbalize the movement sequence:
For example, for side kick:
      1) Turn sideways.
      2) Knee up.
      3) Stretch the leg.
      4) Hold it.
      5) Adjust my stance.
      6) Hold it as long as I can.
      7) Return to fighting stance.

2. Discover what makes your body tick. Is it your torso, your head, your brain, or the angle of your chambered leg that is most influential for initiating each kick?

3. Empty your mind: Does your consciousness hinder your performance? Are you attached to negative feelings about what's going to happen? Then, forget them. Start fresh. Don't think. Pay attention only to each kicking sequence and fill your mind with the feeling of what happens in your muscles.

4. When you find something that works in your training, immediately repeat it at least 100 times to create muscle memory.

5. Have a quiet, non-active post training moment, such as walking or meditation, to synthesize all you have learned.

MULTIPLE KICKS

A multiple kick is any kick that consists of more than one impact, often with the same leg. The key to successfully executing a multiple kick is distributing your energy properly as a result of understanding which kick is the primary technique. Generally, the initial technique is used to set up or distract the opponent and the final kick is the one that impacts the target powerfully. Practice diligently so you can maintain your balance throughout the kicks, especially if you are standing on leg for the entire technique. At this skill level, a flawless execution is critical. If you lose your balance in the middle of the technique, withdraw immediately and start fresh.

PURPOSE

Multiple kicks are used to overwhelm or confuse an opponent. To be successful, control the distance and pace of the attacks. Your rhythm should be fast but unpredictable. Often flashy techniques like these are ineffective in a hard hitting fight, so know their limits and capitalize on the strengths of multiple kicks, especially the strength of striking multiple targets in quick succession.

KEY POINTS

Coordinate your entire body to promote agility, balance and versatility. Center yourself over your standing leg, keep your torso erect and control your arms for balance.

STRIKING AREA

Ball, toes, blade, heel, bottom of the foot, bottom of the heel, instep, knee

TARGETS

1. groin
2. lower abdomen
3. solar plexus
4. chest
5. neck
6. face
7. temple
8. rib cage
9. knee

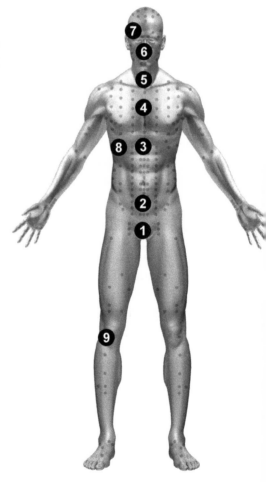

SINGLE LEG LOW-HIGH ROUNDHOUSE KICKS

HOW TO

1. From fighting stance, shift your weight to one leg (front or back according to the situation) and chamber the other leg for roundhouse kick.
2. Throw a low section roundhouse kick, striking the groin or thigh with the instep.
3. Chamber your knee back to position 1 then quickly throw a roundhouse kick to the face, lowering your torso to gain height.

PRACTICE TIP: Focus on the lightning speed of the second kick. The first kick is used to set-up or distract the opponent. To be effective, you need to appear relaxed and disguise your intent.

SINGLE LEG ROUNDHOUSE-WHIP KICKS

HOW TO

1. From fighting stance, shift your weight to one leg (front or back according to the situation) and chamber the other leg for roundhouse kick.
2. Throw a middle section roundhouse kick to the groin or rib cage, striking with the instep.
3. Immediately hook your leg up into a whip kick, striking the face or head with the bottom of your foot while lowering your torso for added height.

PRACTICE TIP: The first kick needs to be horizontal or near-horizontal in order to reverse the kicking direction for the second kick without straining your back. This also helps you stabilize the center of your body for a quick, powerful transition between kicks.

SINGLE LEG DOUBLE SIDE KICKS

HOW TO

1. From fighting stance, shift your weight to one leg (front or back according to the situation) and chamber the other leg for side kick.
2. Throw a side kick to the neck or chest, striking with blade of the foot.
3. Briefly chamber you knee and throw a side kick to the neck while lower your torso to facilitate a high section kick.

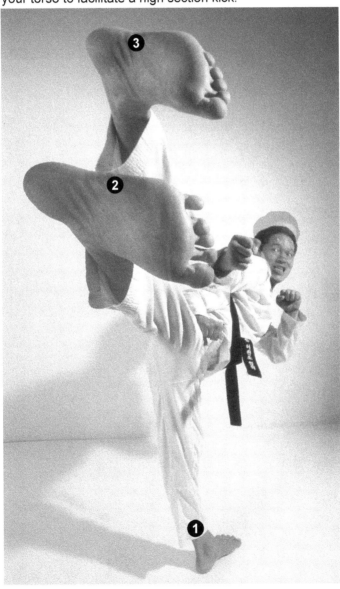

BALANCE POINT

AWARENESS EXERCISE:

Blindfold training heightens your awareness, because the absence of visual cues limits your movement potential. You'll be forced to internalize the movement path of a skill.

Find a safe area, free of obstacles, and try this exercise:

1) Choose one kick to practice (begin with front kick) and observe your movement carefully with your eyes open. You can do this in front of a mirror or simply by visually checking the various parts of your body as you practice.

2) Pay careful attention to the physical patterns of your movement and try to memorize the way you move.

3) Close your eyes (or use a blindfold) and visualize the kick while standing in ready stance.

4) Execute the kick with your eyes closed or blindfolded. Go slowly at first because the lack of visual cues will impair your balance.

5) When you feel comfortable, try kicking a hand-held target while blindfolded. Face the target in fighting stance, note its position and then close your eyes or put your blindfold on. See what happens: is your kick landing where you think it is? Keep practicing until you can hit the target consistently, then try other kicks in the same way.

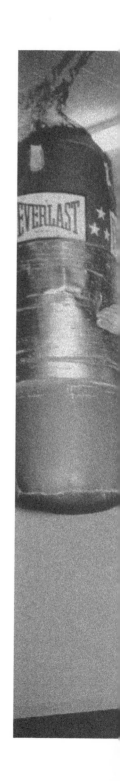

SINGLE LEG HIGH ROUNDHOUSE KICKS

HOW TO

1. From fighting stance, shift your weight to your rear leg and chamber the front leg and throw a roundhouse kick to the face.

2. Retract your leg to a high chamber position and immediately kick to the same target again.

This technique intimidates opponent. Follow up with a cross elbow strike to the face as you step down into fighting stance after kicking.

PRACTICE TIP: Inhale before kicking and then execute both kicks in one exhalation; the first kick is quick and the second kick is powerful.

SINGLE LEG MID-HIGH ROUNDHOUSE KICKS

HOW TO

1. Against a high section roundhouse kick, counter with a middle section roundhouse kick, then drop your foot between you and your opponent.

2. As soon as your opponent's foot lands after kicking and his head rises, throw another roundhouse kick to his face with the same leg.

PRACTICE TIP: Even though you drop your kicking leg between kicks, keep your weight entirely on your supporting leg and create power through your hip rotation between kicks.

SINGLE LEG BACK KICK-WHIP KICK

HOW TO

1. Attack with a back kick to the middle section. Lightly drop your kicking foot, stay close to the opponent and keep your body pivoted slightly away from him.

2. Before he launches his kick, lower your torso and throw a whip kick to the face very quickly. If the opponent moves backward between your kicks, you can slide in before whip kicking.

CAUTION: This technique is not practical unless you are a good in-fighter and very flexible.

SINGLE LEG ROUNDHOUSE-WHIP KICKS

HOW TO

1. Attack with a front or rear leg roundhouse kick to the middle section.
2. As the opponent moves backward, use the same leg to throw a whip kick to the face, striking with the bottom of the foot. There are 3 options between the kicks: you can simply rechamber your leg, drop your foot in front and kick in place, or drop your foot in front and slide in and kick.

TRAINING TIP: The first kick is an intercepting technique. Kick as the opponent moves in to attack.

SINGLE LEG AXE KICK-SIDE KICK

HOW TO

1. Against an opponent who moves to clinch or crowd you, strike the face with an axe kick.

2. Lightly drop your kicking leg in front, keeping your weight to the back of your stance, and when he moves back to evade your kick, pivot your body slightly and quickly thrust out a side kick to his jaw.

TRAINING TIP: When you attack with axe kick, assume your opponent will counterattack with a rear leg roundhouse kick. However he responds, as long as you attack his centerline with a long side kick, you can score or disrupt his attack.

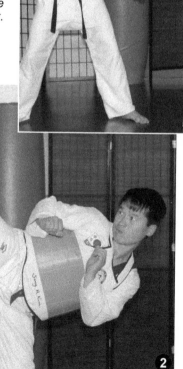

SINGLE LEG ROUNDHOUSE-PUSHING KICKS

HOW TO

1. Counter your opponent's high section roundhouse kick with a middle section roundhouse kick. After kicking, lightly drop your kicking foot right in front of you, keeping your weight to the back of your stance.

2. The instant he tries to kick again, use the same foot to push his rib cage or pelvis with the bottom of the foot.

TRAINING TIP: When you succeed with the pushing kick, knock him down with a jump side kick or jump back kick as he stumbles backward.

SINGLE LEG AXE KICK-ROUNDHOUSE KICKS

HOW TO

1. When your opponent is stalling, throw an axe kick to the face to back him up. After kicking, drop your kicking leg in front of you lightly, keeping your weight more to the back of your stance.

2. As he retreats, pivot your torso and follow up with a powerful middle section roundhouse kick with the same leg.

TRAINING TIP: If he counterattacks with a rear leg back kick after your axe kick, push his hip with the same leg instead of doing a roundhouse kick.

SINGLE LEG TRIPLE KICKS

HOW TO

1. This is a combination that requires agility, strength and coordination. First throw a quick roundhouse kick to the face to create confusion.

2. Re-chamber your kicking leg and immediately do whip kick to the face.

3. Briefly re-chamber your kicking leg then thrust a side kick to the jaw to complete the sequence. Keep your front knee high and your weight on your back leg throughout.

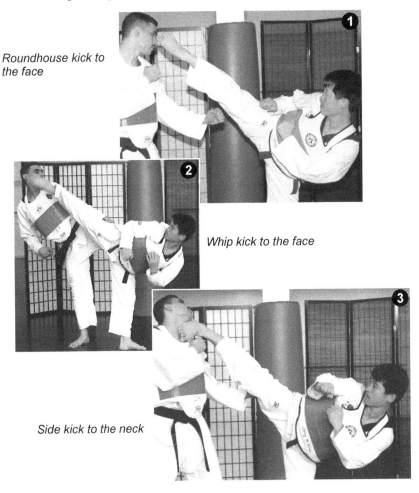

Roundhouse kick to the face

Whip kick to the face

Side kick to the neck

COMBINATION KICKS

A combination is a set of predetermined or random techniques designed to help you unlock the opponent's guard and penetrate his vital areas. It can be orderly or disorderly. In general, a methodical approach, after keen observation of the opponent's behavioral patterns, has a better chance of success than a random or habitual approach. Avoid using repetitive combinations. If you have a favorite combination, change the timing and keep your opponent guessing what the next change might be. That way, you can sustain your superiority.

PURPOSE

Combination kicks are used to put the opponent on the defensive, to set up a calculated response for re-countering, or to compensate for an error in your initial attack. The goal is to continue to have options for initiative attacks so that you can sustain your superiority and win.

KEY POINTS

Choose techniques and targets that build momentum in successive kicks. Be unpredictable. Approach from diverse angles and attack varied targets.

STRIKING AREA

Ball, toes, blade, heel, bottom of the foot, bottom of the heel, instep, knee

TARGETS

1. groin
2. lower abdomen
3. solar plexus
4. chest
5. neck
6. face
7. temple
8. rib cage
9. knee

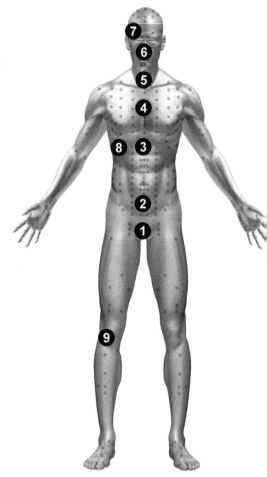

AXE KICK-SPIN WHIP KICK

HOW TO

1. Against a stalling opponent, throw a rear leg axe kick to the face and set your kicking leg down in front.

2. As your opponent backs up, immediately follow up with a rear leg spinning whip kick to the face.

If he does not back up, punch to the chest or rear elbow strike to the jaw.

TRAINING TIP: When you step down after the axe kick, use your stepping momentum to produce additional force in the spinning whip kick. Perform this combination aggressively, without hesitation.

DOUBLE ROUNDHOUSE KICKS

HOW TO

1. When your opponent attacks with a rear leg roundhouse kick, throw a counter rear leg roundhouse kick and set your kicking foot down at a 45° angle to the opponent's torso.

2. As soon as he drops his foot and prepares to kick again (while he is inhaling), throw a quick roundhouse kick to the rib cage before he lifts his leg to kick.

TRAINING TIP: To succeed with techniques like this involving diagonal movements, you have to outplay your opponent with agile footwork.

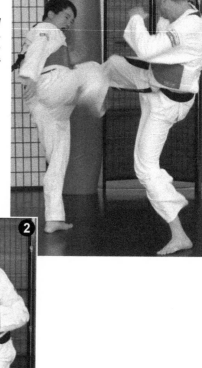

HOP DOUBLE ROUNDHOUSE KICKS

HOW TO

1. When your opponent retreats, hop in, bringing your rear foot forward to close the distance and simultaneously kick the closest target (thigh or ribs).
2. Before your kicking foot lands, throw a roundhouse kick to the lower abdomen with your other leg. The power in this combination comes from pivoting your full body weight around your first kicking leg while in the air.

TRAINING TIP: In double kicking, your legs work like a scissors. Use your body's falling momentum to create maximum power in the second kick.

AXE KICK-ROUNDHOUSE KICK

HOW TO

1. Throw a rear leg axe kick to the face and step down in front. When you attack with axe kick, the opponent has two options: retreat or retaliate.

2. If he retreats, follow up with a powerful rear leg middle section roundhouse kick to his abdomen.

TRAINING TIP: If your opponent doesn't retreat and instead counters with his rear leg, block it with your forearm and punch to the chest to make space between you. Then follow up with a rear leg roundhouse kick to the trunk or face.

ROUNDHOUSE KICK-JUMP SPIN WHIP KICK

HOW TO

1. Throw a powerful rear leg roundhouse kick to the stomach and step down in front. Generally an opponent will crouch in pain or stand up suddenly to expand his ribs and try to catch his breath.

2. If he stands up tall to breathe, jump and throw a rear leg spinning whip kick to the head.

TRAINING TIP: If your opponent bends forward after your first kick, throw a roundhouse kick to the face or neck with the same leg.

TRIPLE ROUNDHOUSE KICKS

HOW TO

1. Execute all three kicks in one breath. First, counterattack with rear leg roundhouse kick against rear leg roundhouse kick. Step down at a 45° angle to the opponent.

2. As the opponent's foot lands and he inhales, throw a roundhouse kick to his rib cage with your other leg.

3. Before setting your kicking leg down, launch a roundhouse kick to the solar plexus with your standing leg (hopping double roundhouse kick).

TRAINING TIP: The purpose of the first kick is to penetrate your opponent's defense and make him move backwards or go on defense. The second and third kicks should be done before he can recover and counterattack.

✱ BALANCE POINT

RULE OF ELIMINATION:

A lack of balance in your combination kicks indicates two possible problems: something is disrupting your gravitational center or your base is weak.

Solutions: Eliminate bad habits and make minute changes to establish better habits.

Try the following exercises:

1. From a squat, jump up, turn around and land in the same position in one motion.

2. Draw a straight line on the floor and practice combination kicking moving along the line to enhance your sense of your center of gravity.

3. Practice the combination in extreme slow motion, holding each kick extended for 30 seconds or until you lose your balance. When you lose balance, move on to the next kick in the combination. Notice how your standing leg and your posture affect your kicks

4. To focus on improving your transitions between kicks, practice the combination using only kick chambers instead of full kicks. For each kick, quickly raise your knee to the chamber position and then step down and quickly proceed to the next movement in the combination.

✴ BALANCE POINT

PUTTING IT ALL TOGETHER:

1. Keep your head upright.

2. Look at the target from start to finish.

3. Check your body alignment.

4. Practice a variety of stances for different techniques.

5. Pay attention to details while you are moving to eliminate unnecessary motions that hinder performance.

6. Keep your knees relaxed and flexed—don't lock them out.

7. Stay relaxed to conserve energy.

8. Utilize gravity wisely.

9. Maximize the principle of reaction force: left vs. right and upward vs. downward movement for balance and power.

10. Always stabilize your initial movement for the best leverage, then let it go.

11. For spin kicks, pivot both feet before kicking, chamber the knee, spot the target, keep your standing knee slightly bent, and let the kick be released instead of kicking with a lot of force. Let things happen and go along with them. When you begin well, you'll finish well.

COMBINATION KICK SAMPLES

1) Right foot roundhouse kick to the trunk
>   + left foot roundhouse kick to the trunk
>   + left foot roundhouse kick to the face
>   + left foot axe kick to the face
>   + right foot roundhouse kick to the trunk
>   + left foot back kick to the trunk
>   + left foot turn kick to the trunk,
>   + forward footwork + right foot back kick to the trunk

2) Forward footwork (one step forward)
>   + back kick to the trunk
>   + roundhouse to the trunk/face
>   + spin whip kick to the face
>   + axe kick to the face

3) Backward footwork (one step back)
>   + back kick to the trunk
>   + roundhouse to the trunk/face
>   + spin whip kick to the face

4) Lateral footwork (one step to the side)
>   + roundhouse to the trunk/face
>   + back kick to the trunk
>   + axe kick to the face

5) Turning footwork (turn your rear foot backward around to the front)
>   + roundhouse kick to the trunk/face
>   + whip kick to the face
>   + spin whip kick to the face

6) Drawing footwork (pull your front foot toward you)
>   + front foot axe kick to the face
>   + front foot whip kick to the face
>   + roundhouse kick (either leg) to the trunk/face

ABOUT THE AUTHOR

Sang H. Kim is the creator of Power Breathing for Life. He is the author of international bestsellers *Ultimate Flexibility, Ultimate Fitness Through Martial Arts,* and *1001 Ways to Motivate Yourself and Others.* His books have been translated into 22 languages. He has been featured or reviewed in Hartford Current, San Francisco Sun Reporter, Innerself Magazine, The Observer, The New York Times, El Nacional, Dallas Observer, Donga Newspaper-Seoul, Chosun Daily-Seoul, Delta Sky, Fighter's Magazine-UK, Cumbernauld Gazette-Scotland, Memphis Business Journal and hundreds more publications.

An internationally respected authority on health and fitness and martial arts training, Sang H. Kim has taught tens of thousands of students in seminars and workshops in North America, Europe, and Asia. He is a certified 8th degree black belt and martial arts instructor as well as the holder of an MS degree in Sports Science and Ph.D. in Exercise Science.

INDEX